A WHO HQ GRAPHIC NOVEL

What Was the
Point of the Civil War?

ALFRED WAUD GOES TO GETTYSBURG

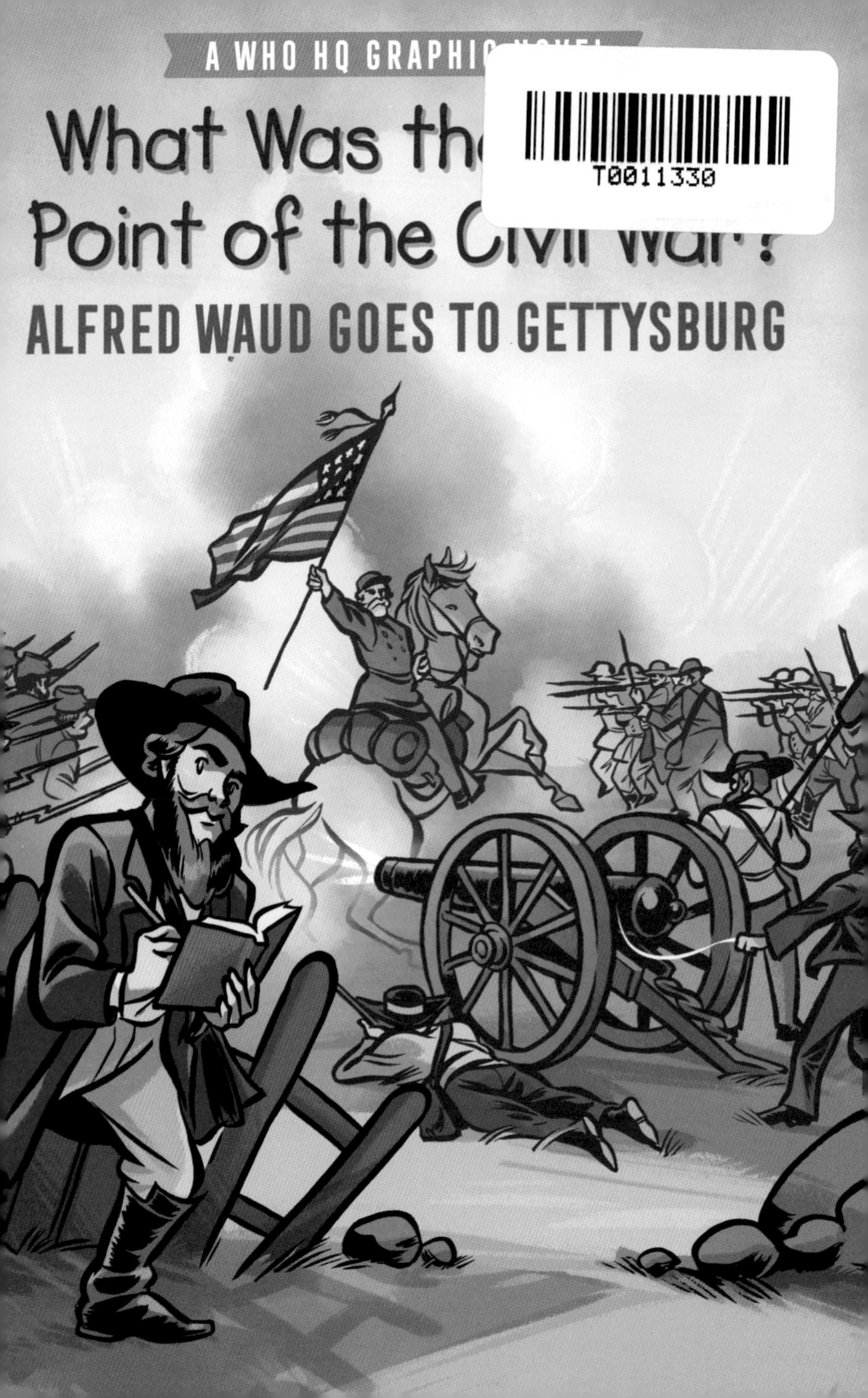

For Matt, whose enthusiasm for history
inspires me every day—ETC

PENGUIN WORKSHOP
An imprint of Penguin Random House LLC, New York

First published in the United States of America by Penguin Workshop,
an imprint of Penguin Random House LLC, New York, 2022

Visit us online at penguinrandomhouse.com.

Library of Congress Cataloging-in-Publication Data is available.

Printed in China

ISBN 9780593225165 (pbk)
ISBN 9780593225172 (hc)

10 9 8 7 6 5 4 3 2 HH
10 9 8 7 6 5 4 3 2 1 WOR

Lettering by Comicraft
Design by Jay Emmanuel

This is a work of nonfiction. All of the events that unfold in the narrative
are rooted in historical fact. Some dialogue and characters have been fictionalized
in order to illustrate or teach a historical point.

The publisher does not have any control over and does not assume any
responsibility for author or third-party websites or their content.

For more information about your favorite historical figures, places, and events,
please visit whohq.com.

A WHO HQ GRAPHIC NOVEL

What Was the Turning Point of the Civil War?

ALFRED WAUD GOES TO GETTYSBURG

by Ellen T. Crenshaw

Penguin Workshop

Introduction

In 1860, Abraham Lincoln was elected president of the United States. This made Southern states angry because Lincoln was antislavery. People who are enslaved have no rights and work for no pay. They are owned and treated like property. Northern states had abandoned slavery; their economy relied on people who worked in factories and businesses. The Southern economy, however, was built on the enslaved labor of Black Americans who worked mostly on small farms. Others labored on massive farms called plantations. Southerners decided they would rather fight than free their enslaved people.

A handful of Southern states seceded from (decided to leave) the United States, calling themselves the Confederate States of America. This divided the country into the North and South. Those who remained loyal to the United States were called the Union. In 1861, Confederate forces fired on Fort Sumter in South Carolina, and the American Civil War began.

Two years later, in June 1863, General George G. Meade was made the new commander of the Union's primary eastern force, the Army of the Potomac. He led more than eighty thousand Union troops on a long and hard march in

pursuit of the Confederate Army of Northern Virginia and its commander, General Robert E. Lee. Lee had invaded Union territory. Meade had to stop Lee before he captured his target: Harrisburg, Pennsylvania, the state capital and an important Union training and supply center. One crucial Confederate victory here could end the Civil War and tear the United States apart.

Under General Lee's leadership, the Confederates (also called Rebels) felt unstoppable. In late 1862 and early 1863, they won two major victories against the Union, in Fredericksburg and Chancellorsville, Virginia. Lee said his soldiers were "the finest body of men that ever tramped the earth." While the Union army outnumbered the Confederates, it had yet to match its opponents in combat.

But the Union troops did have a curious traveler with them. Alfred R. Waud (say: wode), an English immigrant, was a newspaper artist in New York City when the Civil War began. His paper assigned him to follow the Army of the Potomac and report on events through illustrations. He was trailing General Meade when the enemy was discovered in Gettysburg, Pennsylvania.

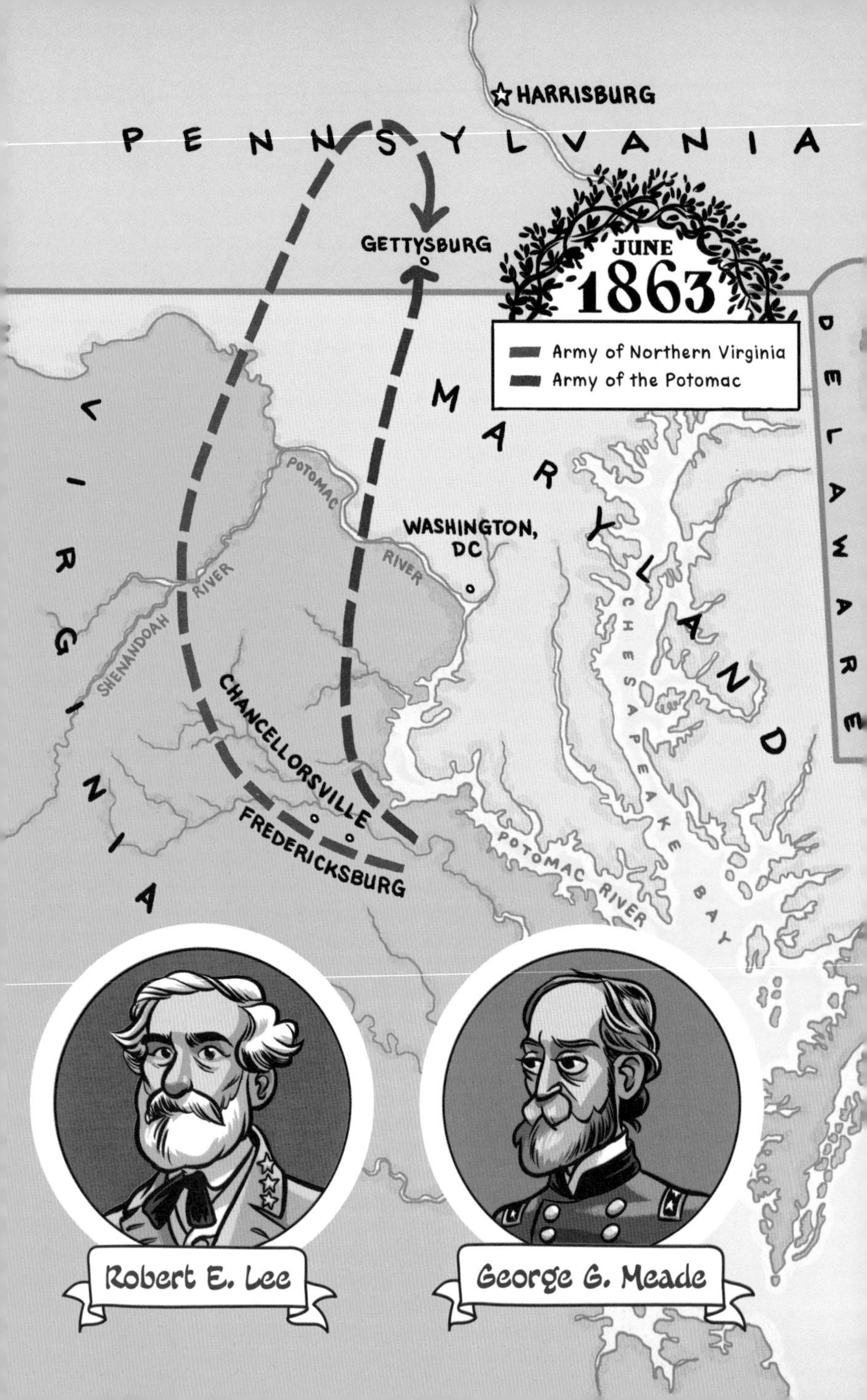
HARRISBURG
PENNSYLVANIA
GETTYSBURG
JUNE
1863
Army of Northern Virginia
Army of the Potomac
DELAWARE
MARYLAND
VIRGINIA
POTOMAC RIVER
WASHINGTON, DC
SHENANDOAH RIVER
CHANCELLORSVILLE
FREDERICKSBURG
POTOMAC RIVER
CHESAPEAKE BAY
Robert E. Lee
George G. Meade

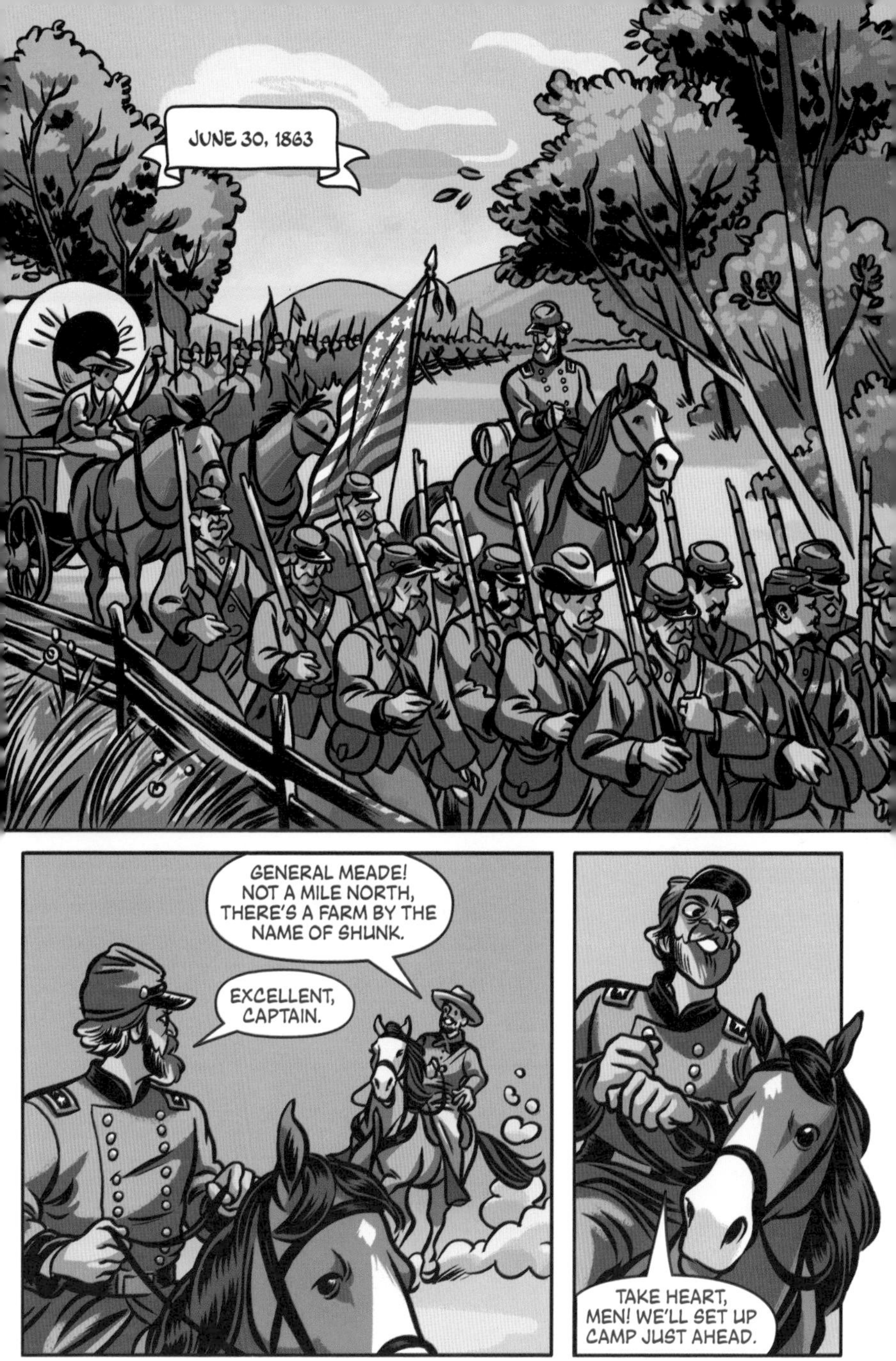
JUNE 30, 1863
GENERAL MEADE! NOT A MILE NORTH, THERE'S A FARM BY THE NAME OF SHUNK.
EXCELLENT, CAPTAIN.
TAKE HEART, MEN! WE'LL SET UP CAMP JUST AHEAD.

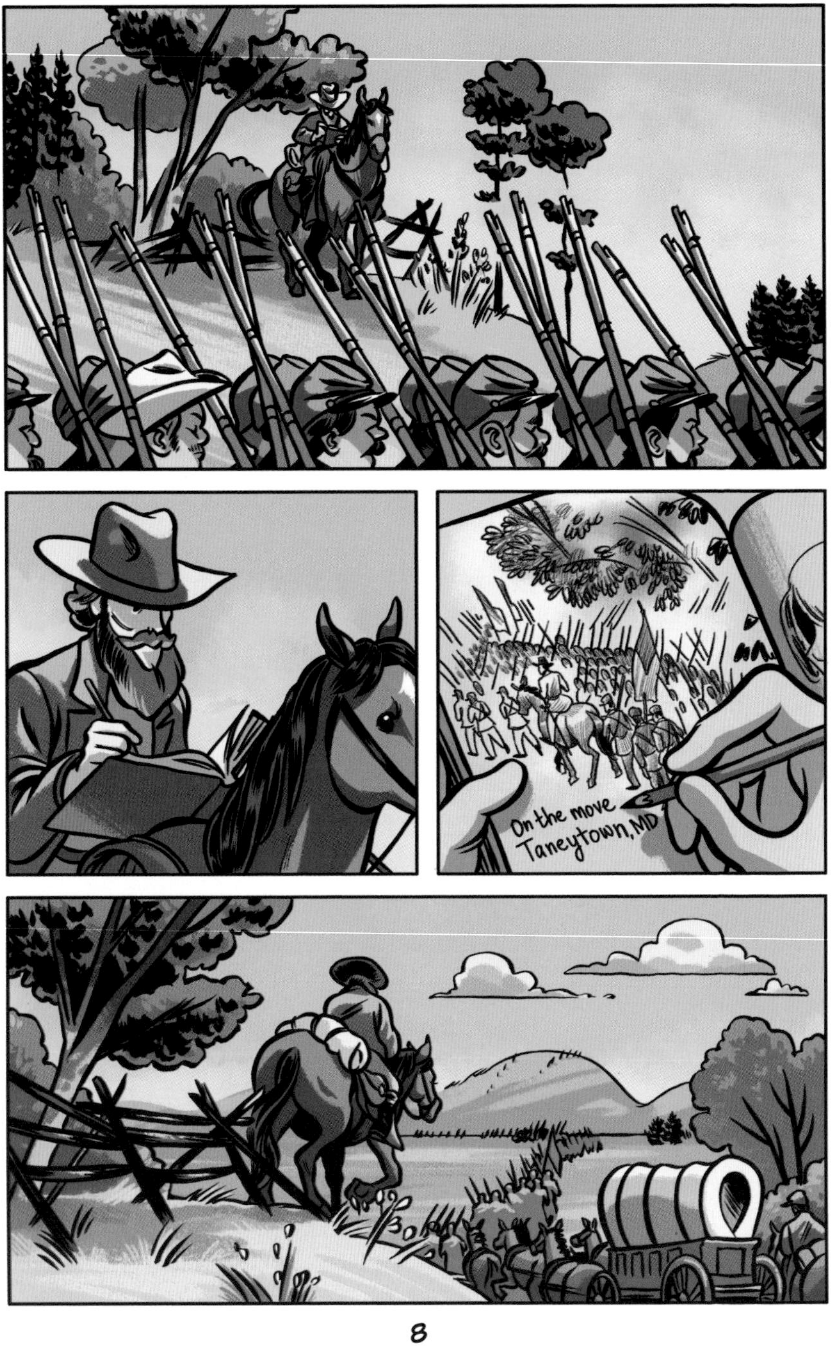
On the move
Taneytown, MD

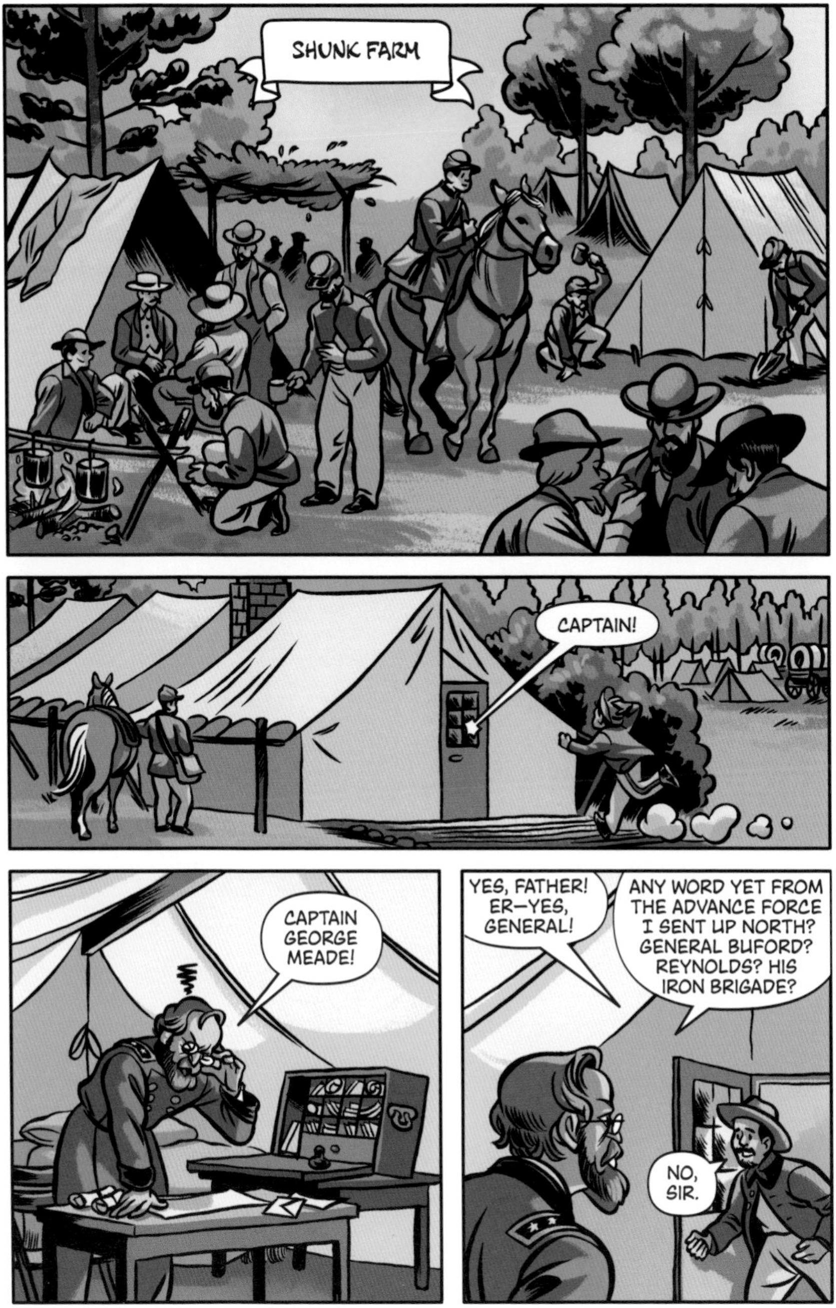
SHUNK FARM
CAPTAIN!
CAPTAIN GEORGE MEADE!
YES, FATHER! ER—YES, GENERAL!
ANY WORD YET FROM THE ADVANCE FORCE I SENT UP NORTH? GENERAL BUFORD? REYNOLDS? HIS IRON BRIGADE?
NO, SIR.

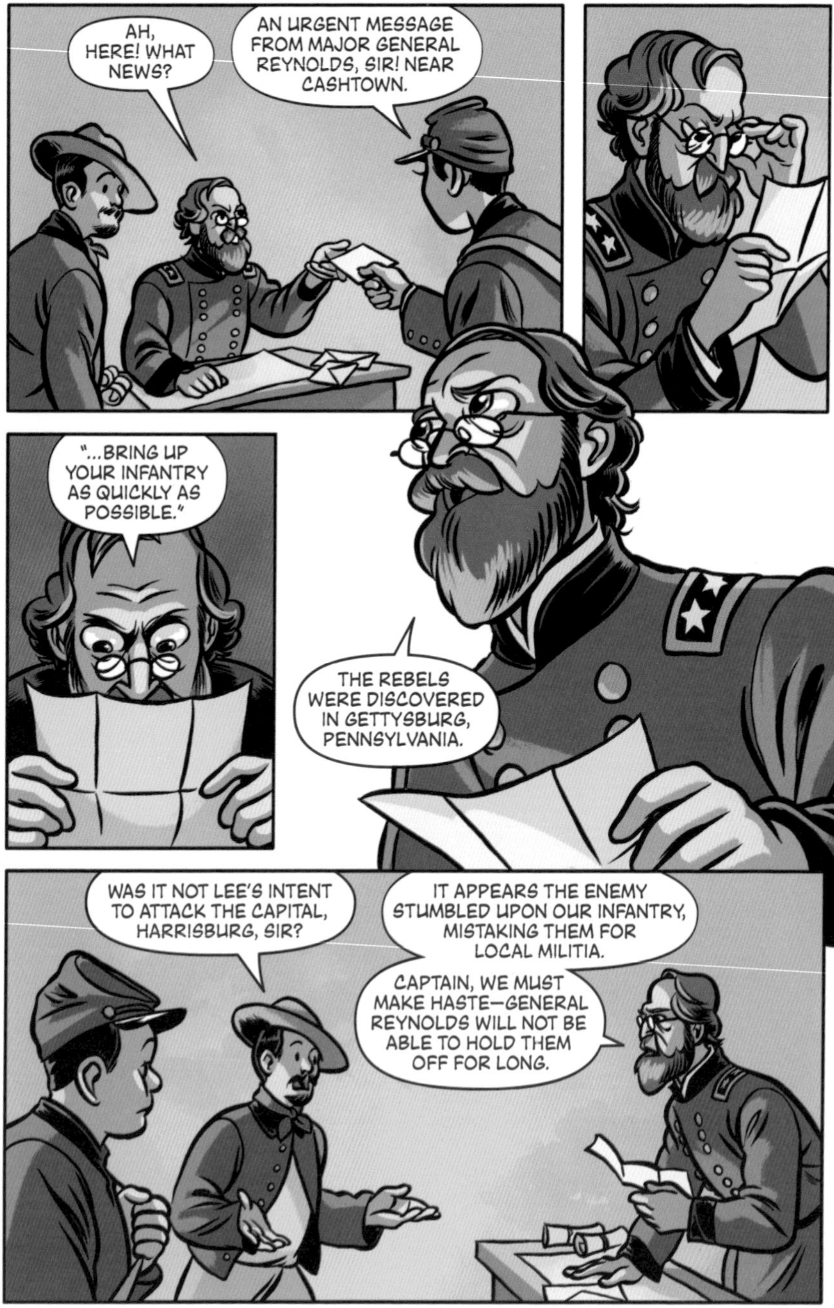
AH, HERE! WHAT NEWS?
AN URGENT MESSAGE FROM MAJOR GENERAL REYNOLDS, SIR! NEAR CASHTOWN.
"...BRING UP YOUR INFANTRY AS QUICKLY AS POSSIBLE."
THE REBELS WERE DISCOVERED IN GETTYSBURG, PENNSYLVANIA.
WAS IT NOT LEE'S INTENT TO ATTACK THE CAPITAL, HARRISBURG, SIR?
IT APPEARS THE ENEMY STUMBLED UPON OUR INFANTRY, MISTAKING THEM FOR LOCAL MILITIA.
CAPTAIN, WE MUST MAKE HASTE—GENERAL REYNOLDS WILL NOT BE ABLE TO HOLD THEM OFF FOR LONG.

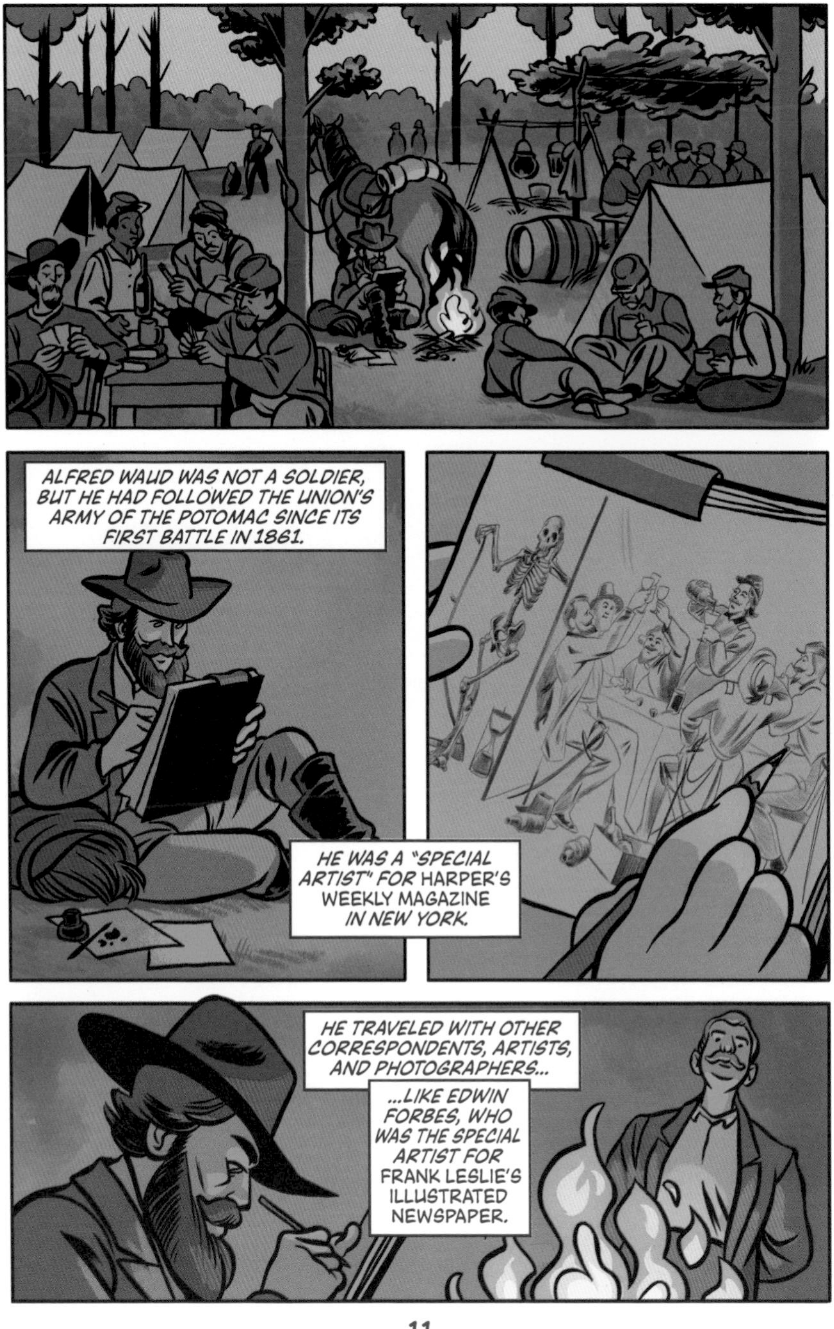
ALFRED WAUD WAS NOT A SOLDIER, BUT HE HAD FOLLOWED THE UNION'S ARMY OF THE POTOMAC SINCE ITS FIRST BATTLE IN 1861.
HE WAS A "SPECIAL ARTIST" FOR HARPER'S WEEKLY MAGAZINE IN NEW YORK.
HE TRAVELED WITH OTHER CORRESPONDENTS, ARTISTS, AND PHOTOGRAPHERS...
...LIKE EDWIN FORBES, WHO WAS THE SPECIAL ARTIST FOR FRANK LESLIE'S ILLUSTRATED NEWSPAPER.

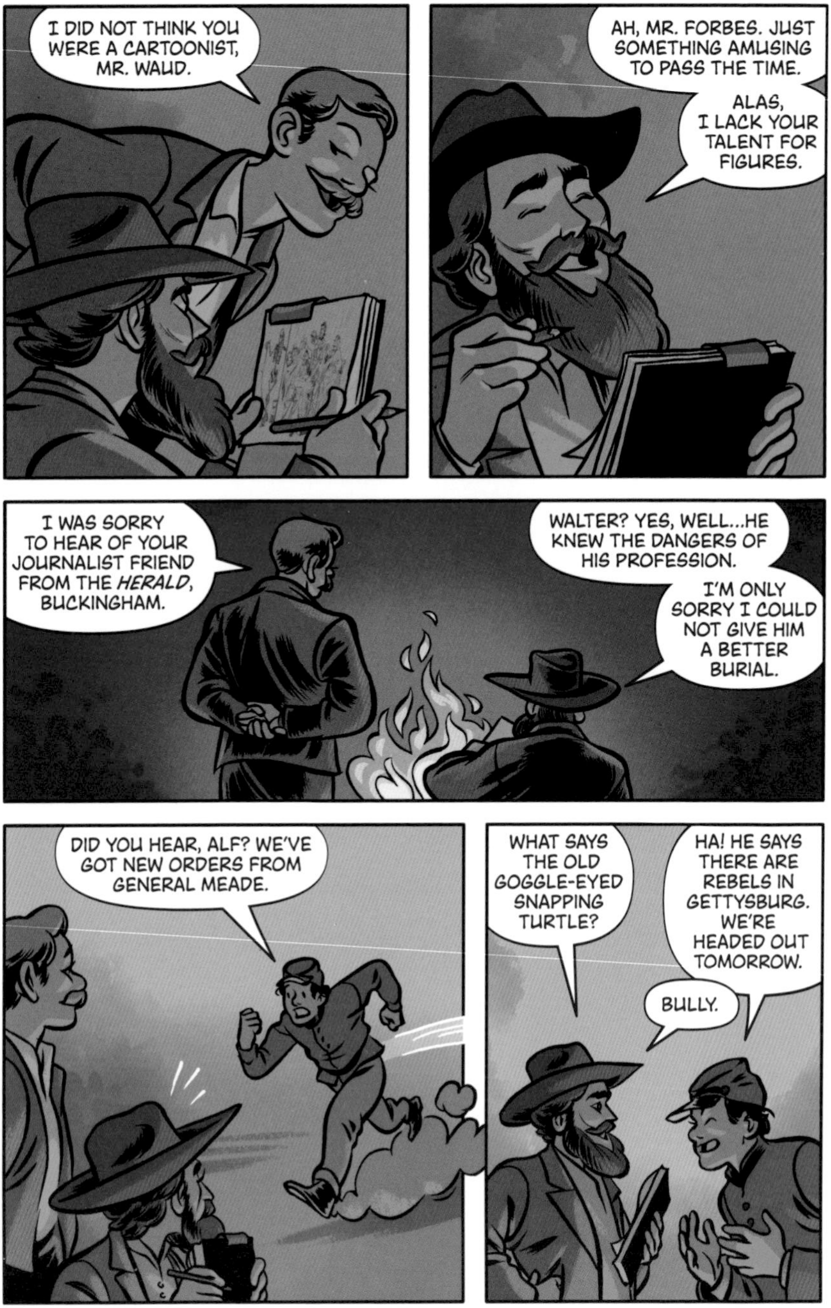
I DID NOT THINK YOU WERE A CARTOONIST, MR. WAUD.
AH, MR. FORBES. JUST SOMETHING AMUSING TO PASS THE TIME.
ALAS, I LACK YOUR TALENT FOR FIGURES.
I WAS SORRY TO HEAR OF YOUR JOURNALIST FRIEND FROM THE *HERALD*, BUCKINGHAM.
WALTER? YES, WELL...HE KNEW THE DANGERS OF HIS PROFESSION.
I'M ONLY SORRY I COULD NOT GIVE HIM A BETTER BURIAL.
DID YOU HEAR, ALF? WE'VE GOT NEW ORDERS FROM GENERAL MEADE.
WHAT SAYS THE OLD GOGGLE-EYED SNAPPING TURTLE?
HA! HE SAYS THERE ARE REBELS IN GETTYSBURG. WE'RE HEADED OUT TOMORROW.
BULLY.

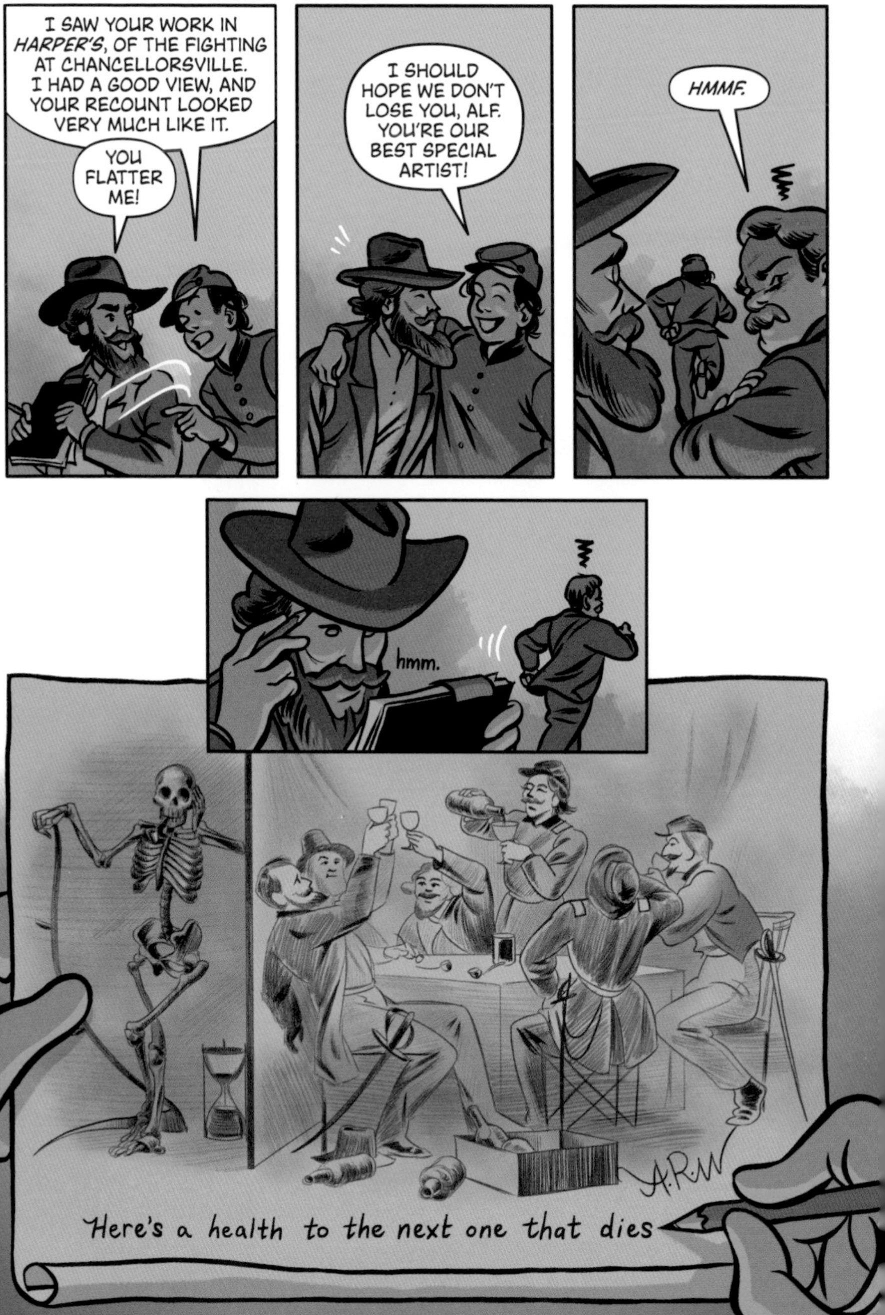
I SAW YOUR WORK IN *HARPER'S*, OF THE FIGHTING AT CHANCELLORSVILLE. I HAD A GOOD VIEW, AND YOUR RECOUNT LOOKED VERY MUCH LIKE IT.
YOU FLATTER ME!
I SHOULD HOPE WE DON'T LOSE YOU, ALF. YOU'RE OUR BEST SPECIAL ARTIST!
HMMF.
hmm.
A.R.W
Here's a health to the next one that dies

What Is a Special Artist?

When the Civil War began, illustrated weekly newspapers sent their staff artists to cover the war fronts. They were called "special artists" or "special correspondents." These artists would follow the Union and Confederate armies on horseback, camp alongside the troops, and draw pictures of what was happening in the war. Their materials included toned papers, paint called gouache in white, black ink, and pencils. A special artist also brought necessary supplies for protection and comfort; for instance, Alf Waud carried a sketchbook, bowie knife, revolver, blanket roll, and flask.

Once a special artist finished a drawing in the field, they sent the illustration by mail, ship, or courier to their newspaper. There, a staff of engravers copied the drawing in pieces, like a puzzle, onto wooden blocks. The blocks were put together to form a complete picture. Then, through a process called electrotype, a perfect metal copy was made of the wood engraving. Finally, the metal copy—called a printing plate—was inked and pressed onto paper. A single plate made more than one hundred thousand prints! The whole process, from sketch to publication, took three to six weeks.

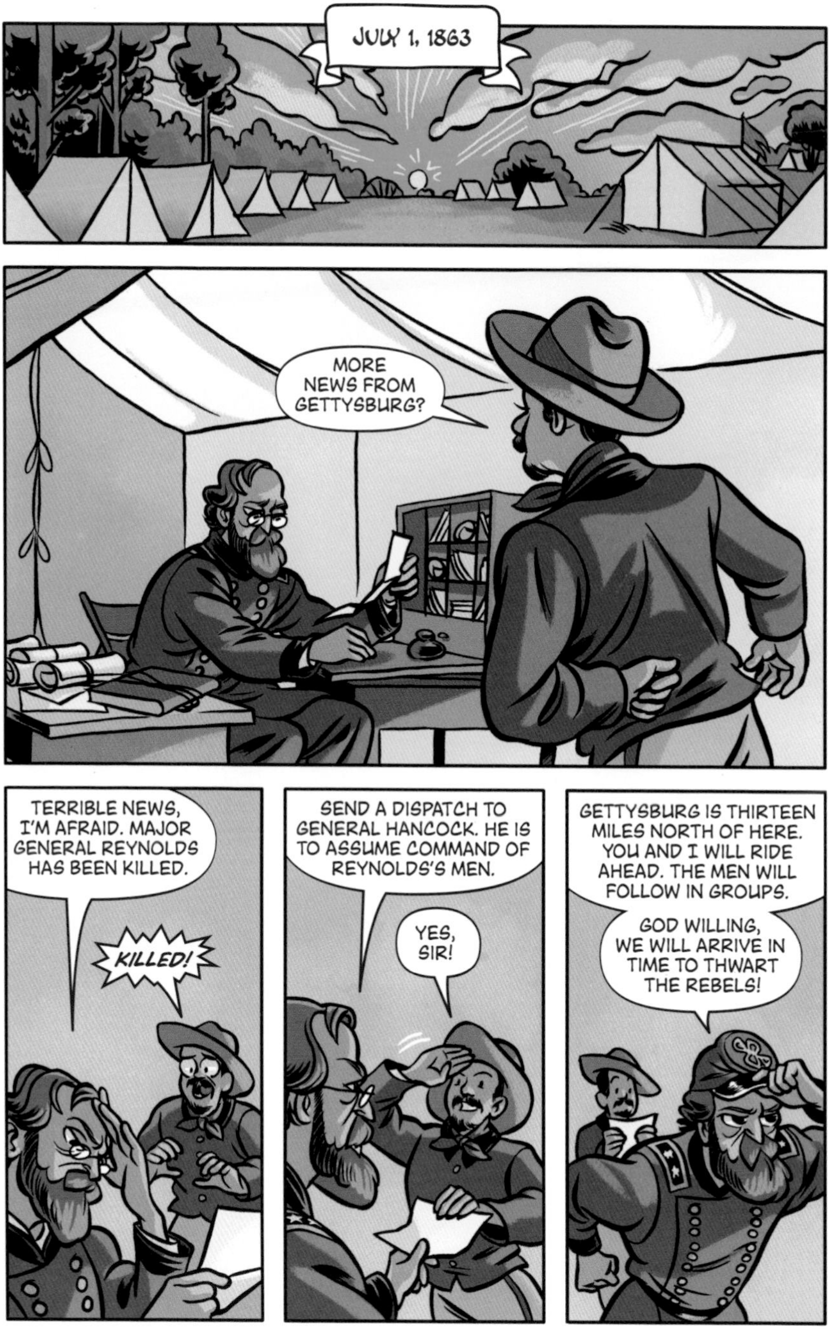
JULY 1, 1863
MORE NEWS FROM GETTYSBURG?
TERRIBLE NEWS, I'M AFRAID. MAJOR GENERAL REYNOLDS HAS BEEN KILLED.
KILLED!
SEND A DISPATCH TO GENERAL HANCOCK. HE IS TO ASSUME COMMAND OF REYNOLDS'S MEN.
YES, SIR!
GETTYSBURG IS THIRTEEN MILES NORTH OF HERE. YOU AND I WILL RIDE AHEAD. THE MEN WILL FOLLOW IN GROUPS.
GOD WILLING, WE WILL ARRIVE IN TIME TO THWART THE REBELS!

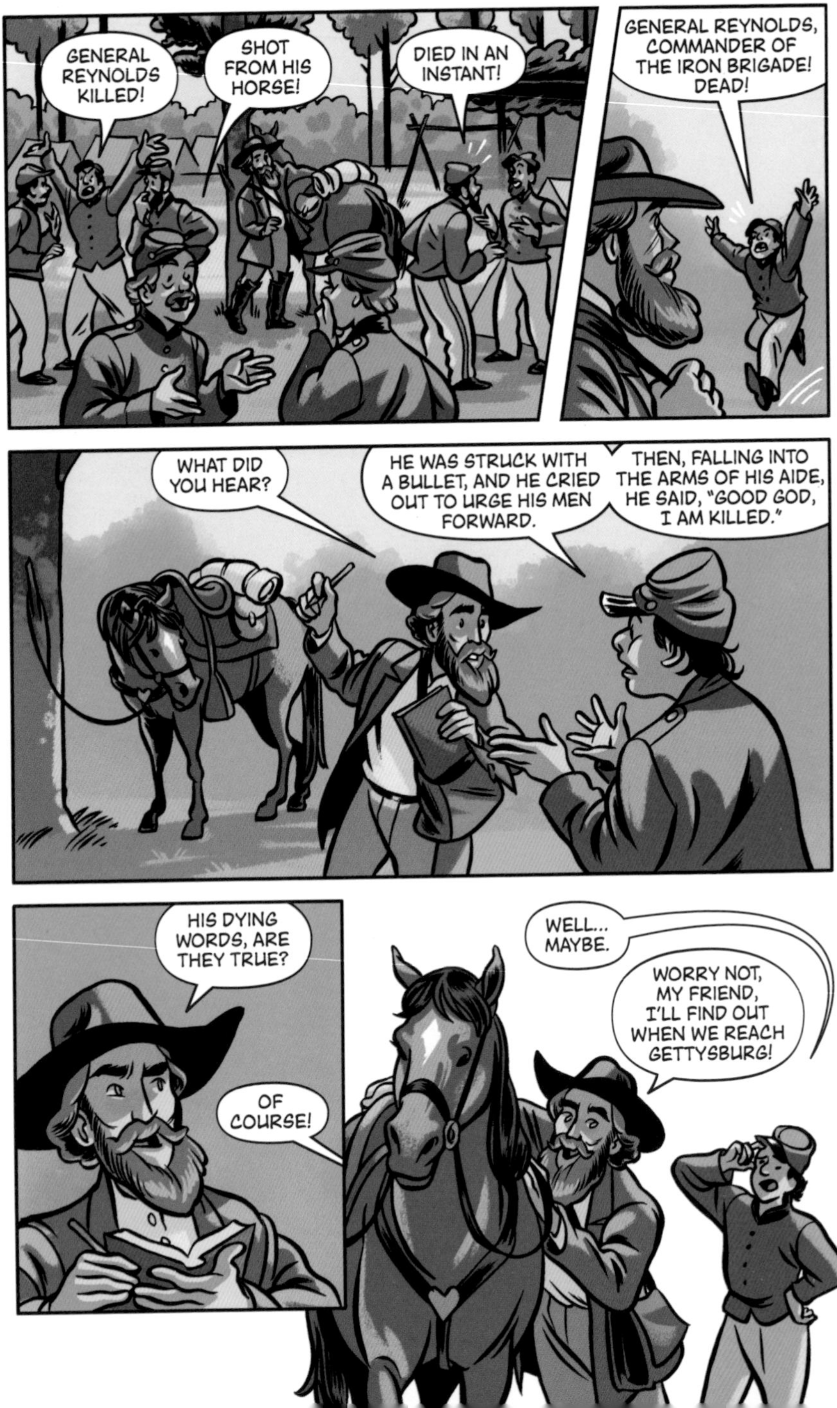
GENERAL REYNOLDS KILLED!
SHOT FROM HIS HORSE!
DIED IN AN INSTANT!
GENERAL REYNOLDS, COMMANDER OF THE IRON BRIGADE! DEAD!
WHAT DID YOU HEAR?
HE WAS STRUCK WITH A BULLET, AND HE CRIED OUT TO URGE HIS MEN FORWARD.
THEN, FALLING INTO THE ARMS OF HIS AIDE, HE SAID, "GOOD GOD, I AM KILLED."
HIS DYING WORDS, ARE THEY TRUE?
OF COURSE!
WELL... MAYBE.
WORRY NOT, MY FRIEND, I'LL FIND OUT WHEN WE REACH GETTYSBURG!

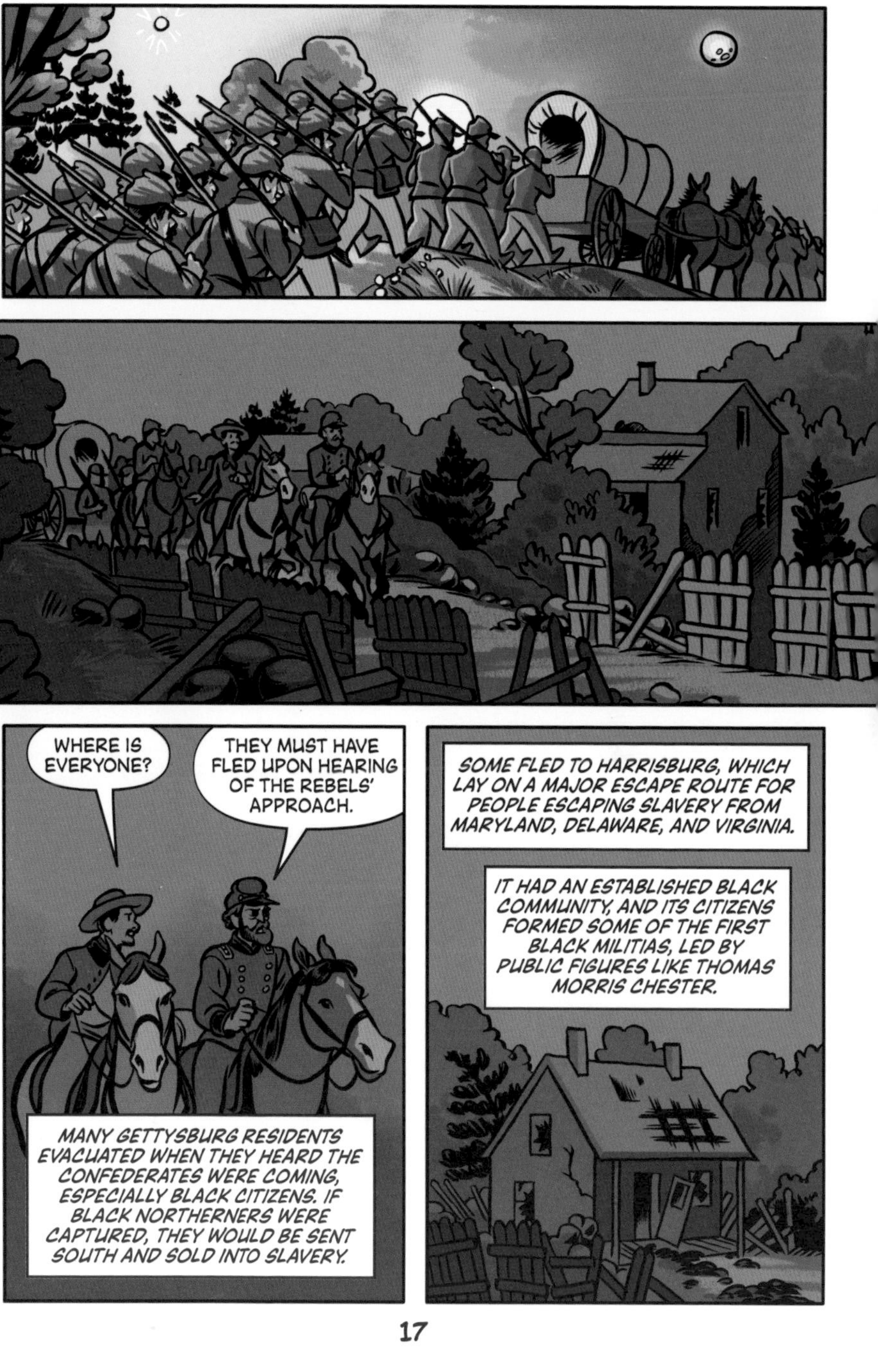
WHERE IS EVERYONE?
THEY MUST HAVE FLED UPON HEARING OF THE REBELS' APPROACH.
MANY GETTYSBURG RESIDENTS EVACUATED WHEN THEY HEARD THE CONFEDERATES WERE COMING, ESPECIALLY BLACK CITIZENS. IF BLACK NORTHERNERS WERE CAPTURED, THEY WOULD BE SENT SOUTH AND SOLD INTO SLAVERY.
SOME FLED TO HARRISBURG, WHICH LAY ON A MAJOR ESCAPE ROUTE FOR PEOPLE ESCAPING SLAVERY FROM MARYLAND, DELAWARE, AND VIRGINIA.
IT HAD AN ESTABLISHED BLACK COMMUNITY, AND ITS CITIZENS FORMED SOME OF THE FIRST BLACK MILITIAS, LED BY PUBLIC FIGURES LIKE THOMAS MORRIS CHESTER.

Thomas Morris Chester

Born on May 11, 1834, Thomas Morris Chester was a prominent Black lawyer in Harrisburg, Pennsylvania. Throughout the Civil War, he urged the Union army to recruit Black soldiers. When Harrisburg came under threat from a possible Confederate invasion, its Black citizens wanted to fight to protect their home. Harrisburg formed two all-Black militias, and Chester was made a captain. Other volunteers went to join the Fifty-Fourth and Fifty-Fifth Massachusetts Regiments, all-Black infantry regiments in the Union army.

In 1864, Chester was hired as a Union war correspondent for the *Philadelphia Press.* Unlike other journalists, he specifically covered Black troops in the field. He criticized cruel white commanders and praised those who treated their men with respect. He wrote, "It seems that the disposition to treat colored persons as if they were human is hard for even some loyal men." He was the only Black reporter on the front lines of the Civil War.

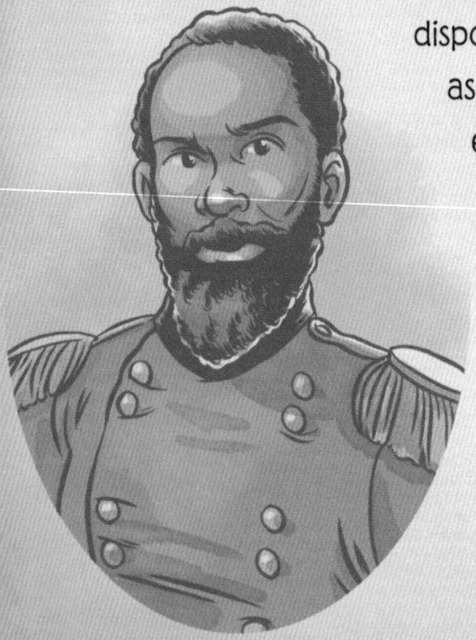

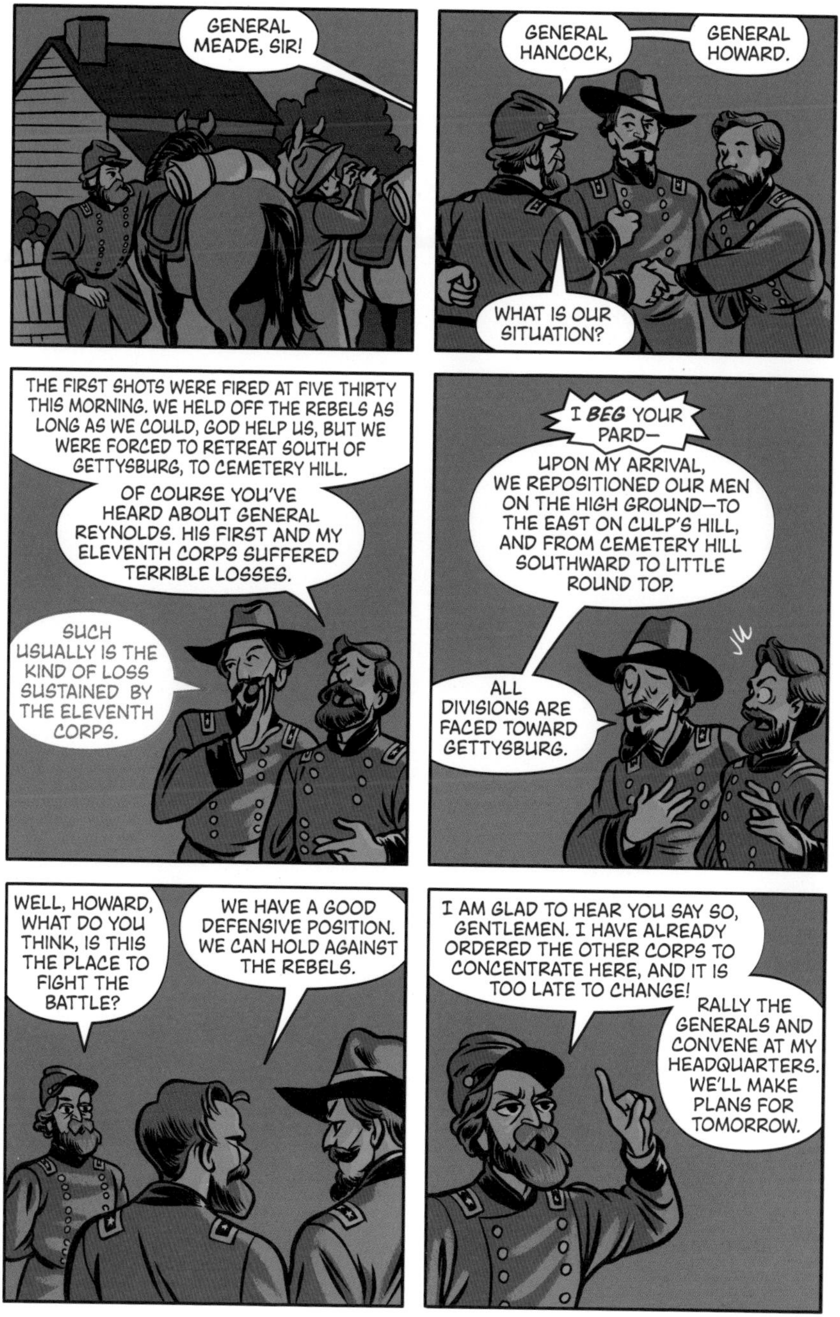
GENERAL MEADE, SIR!
GENERAL HANCOCK,
GENERAL HOWARD.
WHAT IS OUR SITUATION?
THE FIRST SHOTS WERE FIRED AT FIVE THIRTY THIS MORNING. WE HELD OFF THE REBELS AS LONG AS WE COULD, GOD HELP US, BUT WE WERE FORCED TO RETREAT SOUTH OF GETTYSBURG, TO CEMETERY HILL.
OF COURSE YOU'VE HEARD ABOUT GENERAL REYNOLDS. HIS FIRST AND MY ELEVENTH CORPS SUFFERED TERRIBLE LOSSES.
SUCH USUALLY IS THE KIND OF LOSS SUSTAINED BY THE ELEVENTH CORPS.
I **BEG** YOUR PARD—
UPON MY ARRIVAL, WE REPOSITIONED OUR MEN ON THE HIGH GROUND—TO THE EAST ON CULP'S HILL, AND FROM CEMETERY HILL SOUTHWARD TO LITTLE ROUND TOP.
ALL DIVISIONS ARE FACED TOWARD GETTYSBURG.
WELL, HOWARD, WHAT DO YOU THINK, IS THIS THE PLACE TO FIGHT THE BATTLE?
WE HAVE A GOOD DEFENSIVE POSITION. WE CAN HOLD AGAINST THE REBELS.
I AM GLAD TO HEAR YOU SAY SO, GENTLEMEN. I HAVE ALREADY ORDERED THE OTHER CORPS TO CONCENTRATE HERE, AND IT IS TOO LATE TO CHANGE!
RALLY THE GENERALS AND CONVENE AT MY HEADQUARTERS. WE'LL MAKE PLANS FOR TOMORROW.

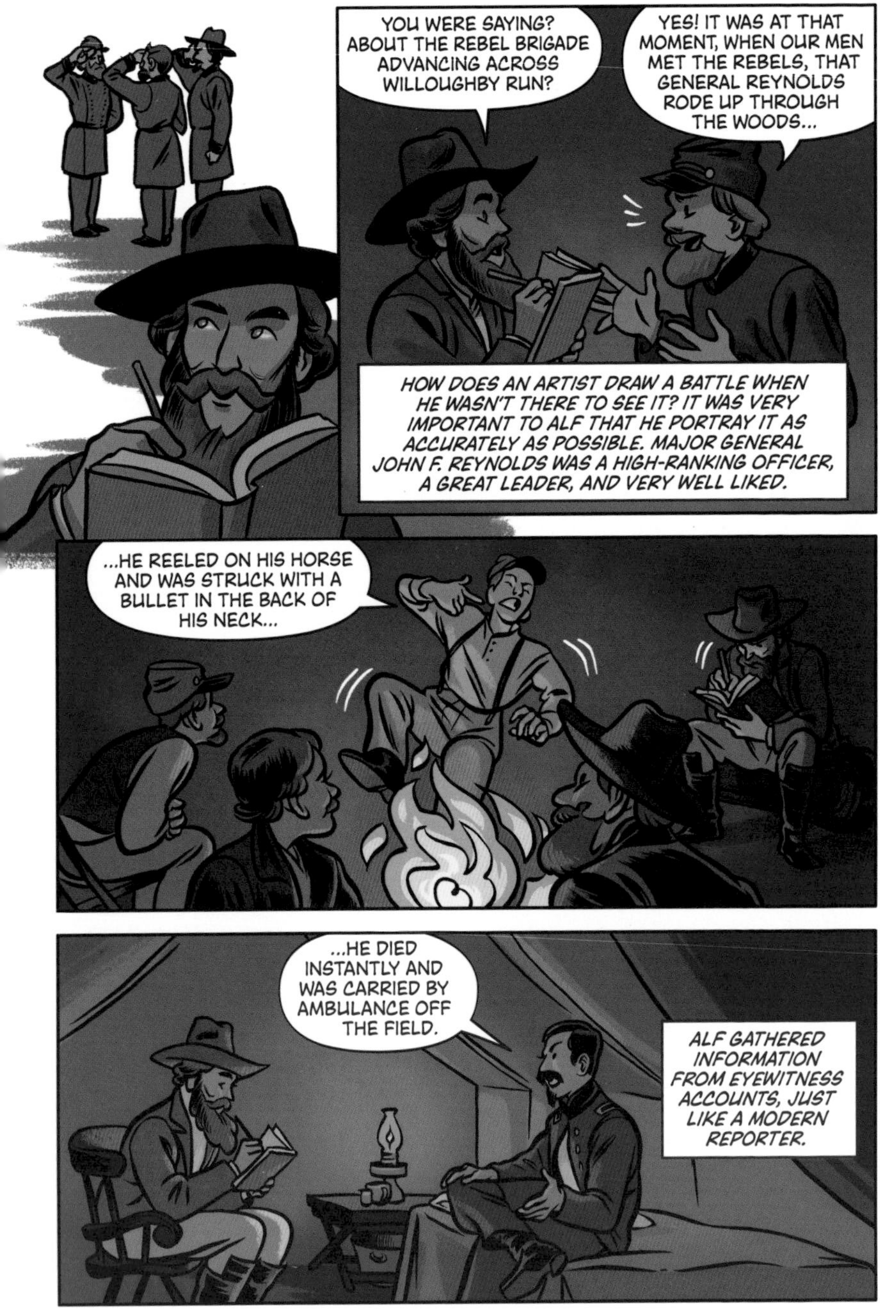
YOU WERE SAYING? ABOUT THE REBEL BRIGADE ADVANCING ACROSS WILLOUGHBY RUN?
YES! IT WAS AT THAT MOMENT, WHEN OUR MEN MET THE REBELS, THAT GENERAL REYNOLDS RODE UP THROUGH THE WOODS...
HOW DOES AN ARTIST DRAW A BATTLE WHEN HE WASN'T THERE TO SEE IT? IT WAS VERY IMPORTANT TO ALF THAT HE PORTRAY IT AS ACCURATELY AS POSSIBLE. MAJOR GENERAL JOHN F. REYNOLDS WAS A HIGH-RANKING OFFICER, A GREAT LEADER, AND VERY WELL LIKED.
...HE REELED ON HIS HORSE AND WAS STRUCK WITH A BULLET IN THE BACK OF HIS NECK...
...HE DIED INSTANTLY AND WAS CARRIED BY AMBULANCE OFF THE FIELD.
ALF GATHERED INFORMATION FROM EYEWITNESS ACCOUNTS, JUST LIKE A MODERN REPORTER.

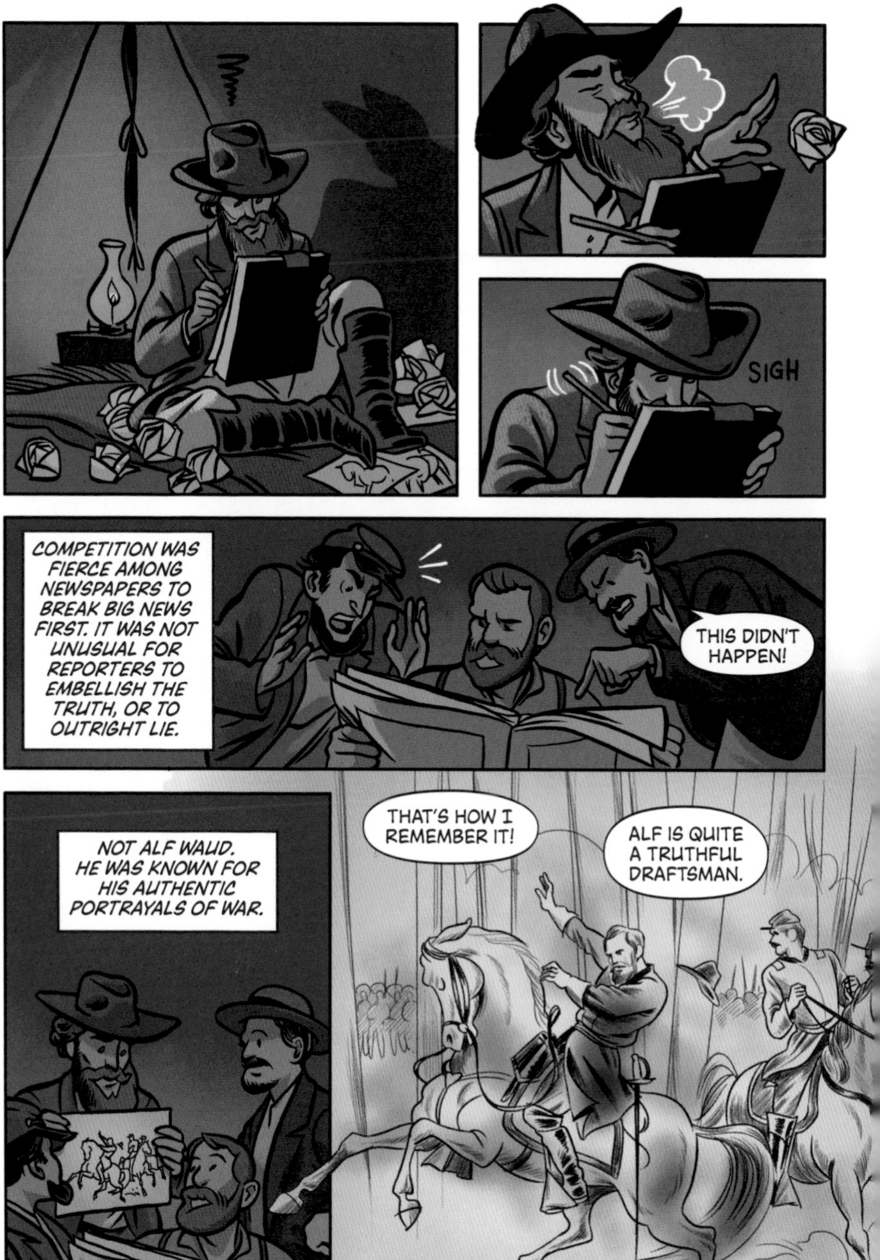
SIGH
COMPETITION WAS FIERCE AMONG NEWSPAPERS TO BREAK BIG NEWS FIRST. IT WAS NOT UNUSUAL FOR REPORTERS TO EMBELLISH THE TRUTH, OR TO OUTRIGHT LIE.
THIS DIDN'T HAPPEN!
NOT ALF WAUD. HE WAS KNOWN FOR HIS AUTHENTIC PORTRAYALS OF WAR.
THAT'S HOW I REMEMBER IT!
ALF IS QUITE A TRUTHFUL DRAFTSMAN.

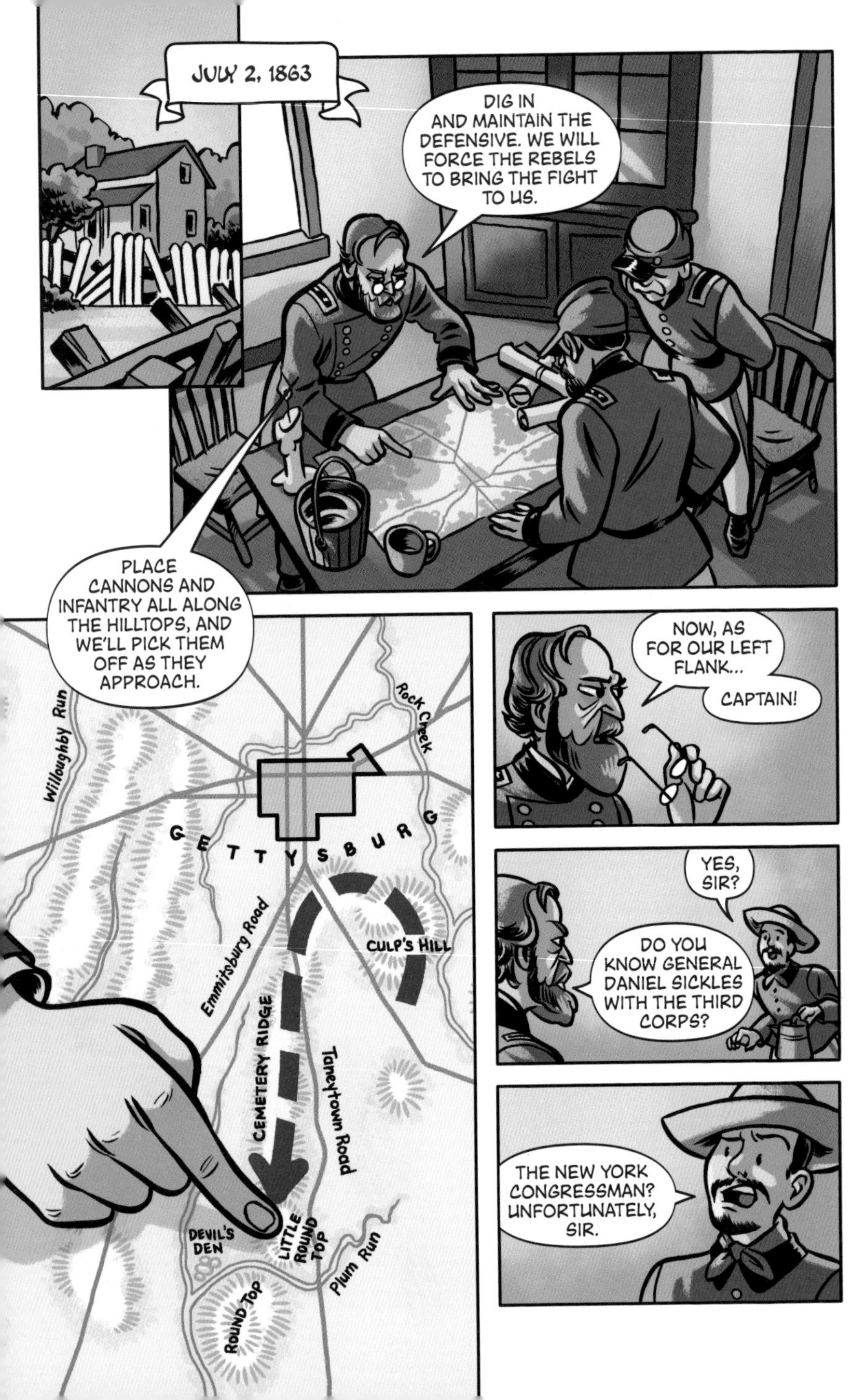
JULY 2, 1863
DIG IN AND MAINTAIN THE DEFENSIVE. WE WILL FORCE THE REBELS TO BRING THE FIGHT TO US.
PLACE CANNONS AND INFANTRY ALL ALONG THE HILLTOPS, AND WE'LL PICK THEM OFF AS THEY APPROACH.
Willoughby Run
Rock Creek
GETTYSBURG
Emmitsburg Road
CULP'S HILL
CEMETERY RIDGE
Taneytown Road
DEVIL'S DEN
LITTLE ROUND TOP
Plum Run
ROUND TOP
NOW, AS FOR OUR LEFT FLANK...
CAPTAIN!
YES, SIR?
DO YOU KNOW GENERAL DANIEL SICKLES WITH THE THIRD CORPS?
THE NEW YORK CONGRESSMAN? UNFORTUNATELY, SIR.

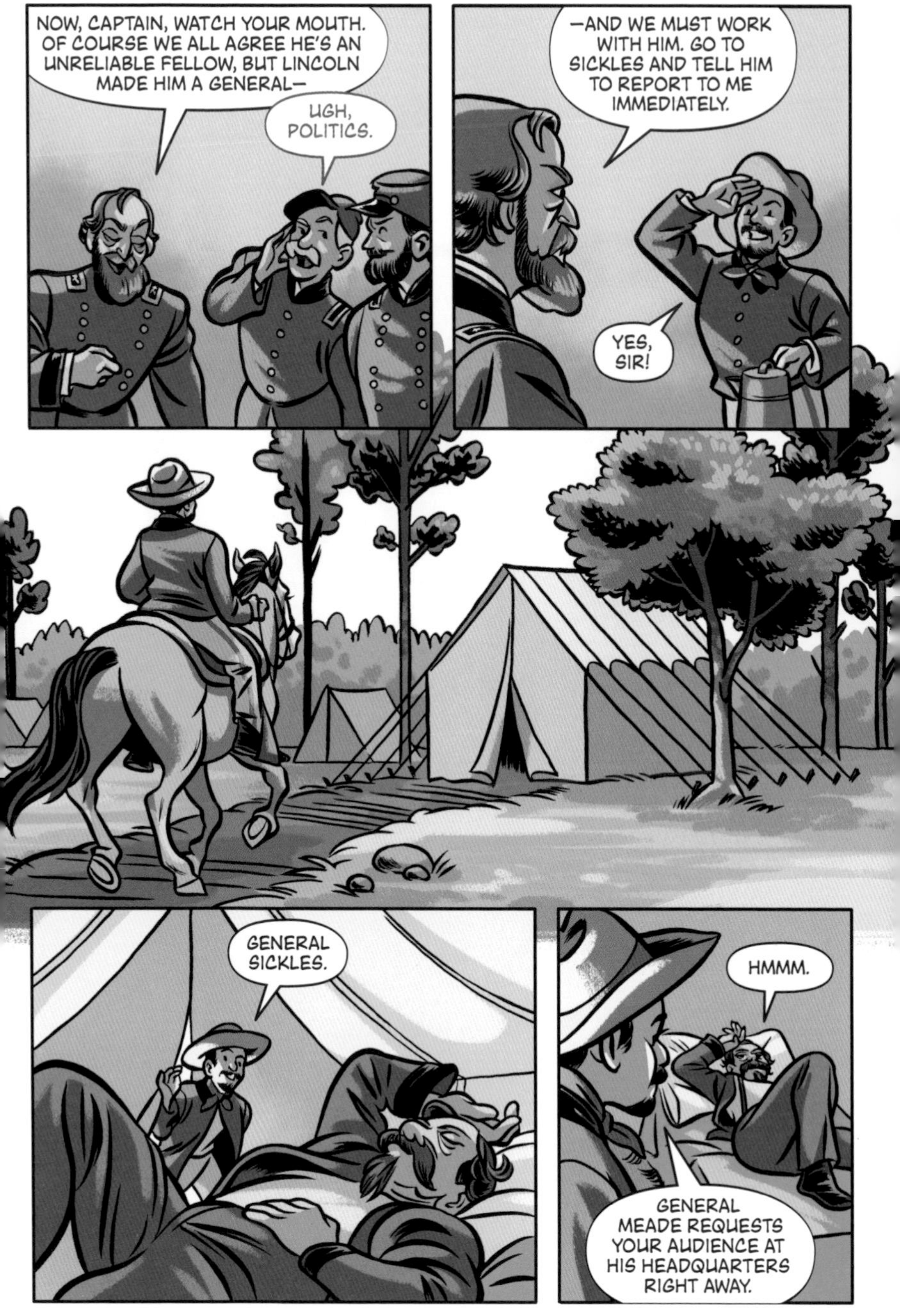
NOW, CAPTAIN, WATCH YOUR MOUTH. OF COURSE WE ALL AGREE HE'S AN UNRELIABLE FELLOW, BUT LINCOLN MADE HIM A GENERAL—
UGH, POLITICS.
—AND WE MUST WORK WITH HIM. GO TO SICKLES AND TELL HIM TO REPORT TO ME IMMEDIATELY.
YES, SIR!
GENERAL SICKLES.
HMMM.
GENERAL MEADE REQUESTS YOUR AUDIENCE AT HIS HEADQUARTERS RIGHT AWAY.

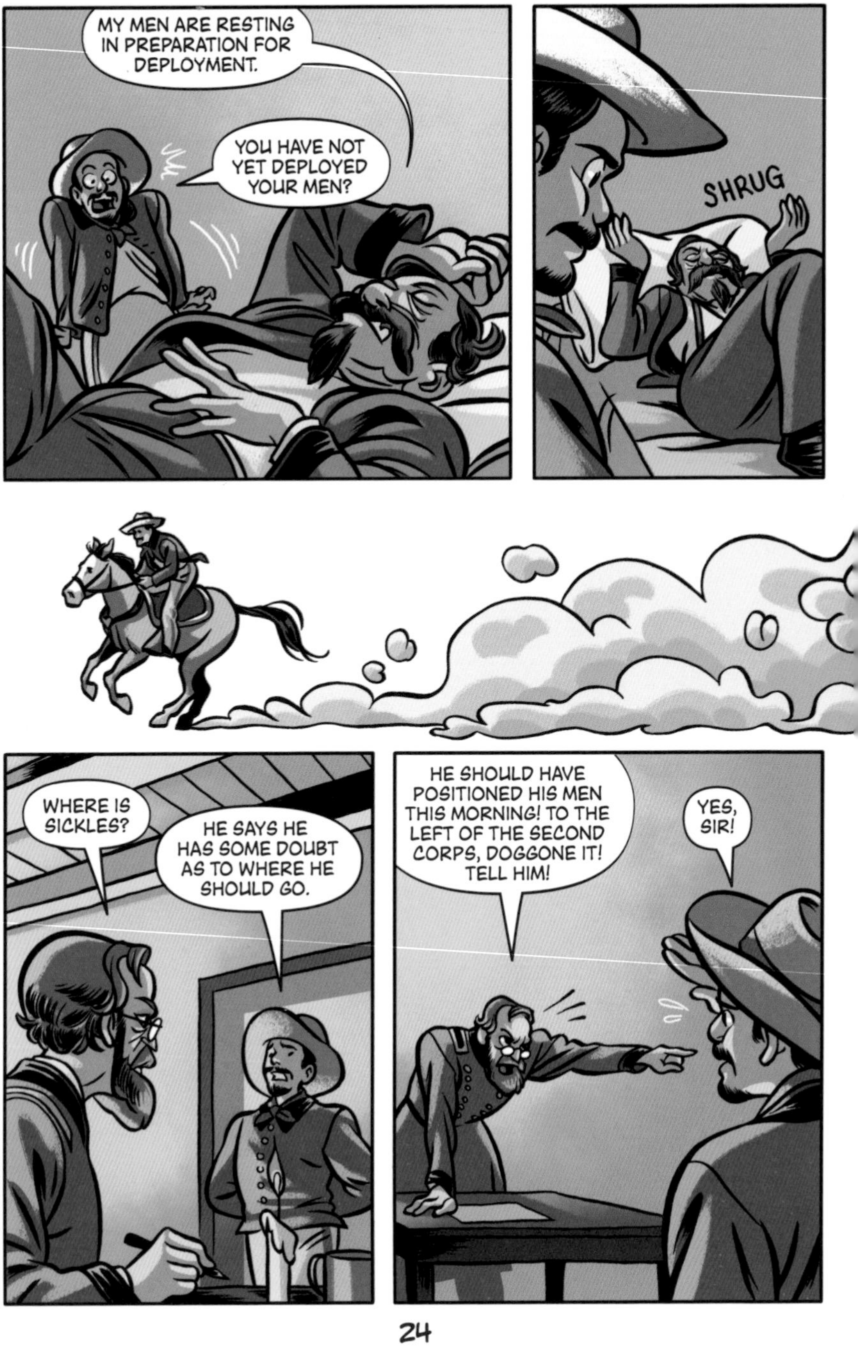
MY MEN ARE RESTING IN PREPARATION FOR DEPLOYMENT.
YOU HAVE NOT YET DEPLOYED YOUR MEN?
SHRUG
WHERE IS SICKLES?
HE SAYS HE HAS SOME DOUBT AS TO WHERE HE SHOULD GO.
HE SHOULD HAVE POSITIONED HIS MEN THIS MORNING! TO THE LEFT OF THE SECOND CORPS, DOGGONE IT! TELL HIM!
YES, SIR!

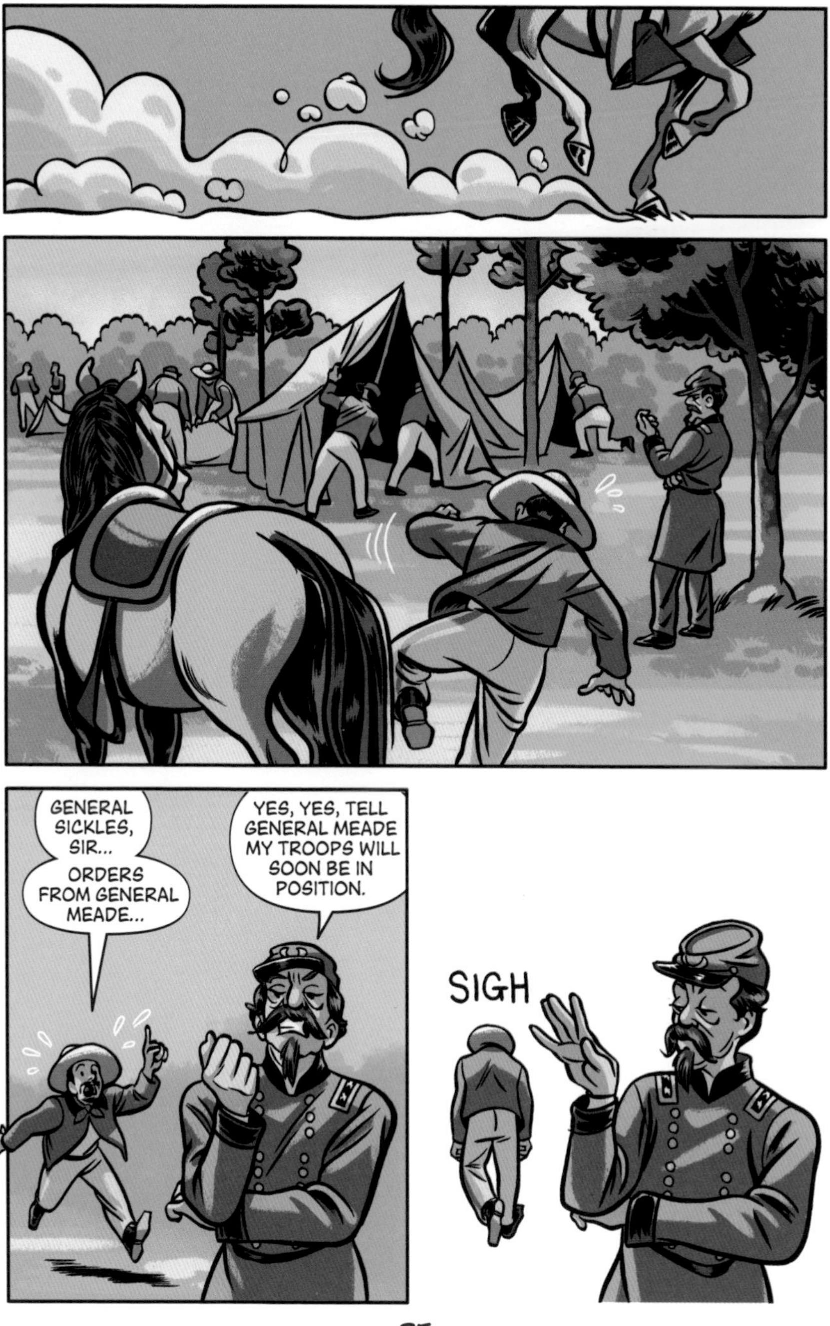
GENERAL SICKLES, SIR...
ORDERS FROM GENERAL MEADE...
YES, YES, TELL GENERAL MEADE MY TROOPS WILL SOON BE IN POSITION.
SIGH

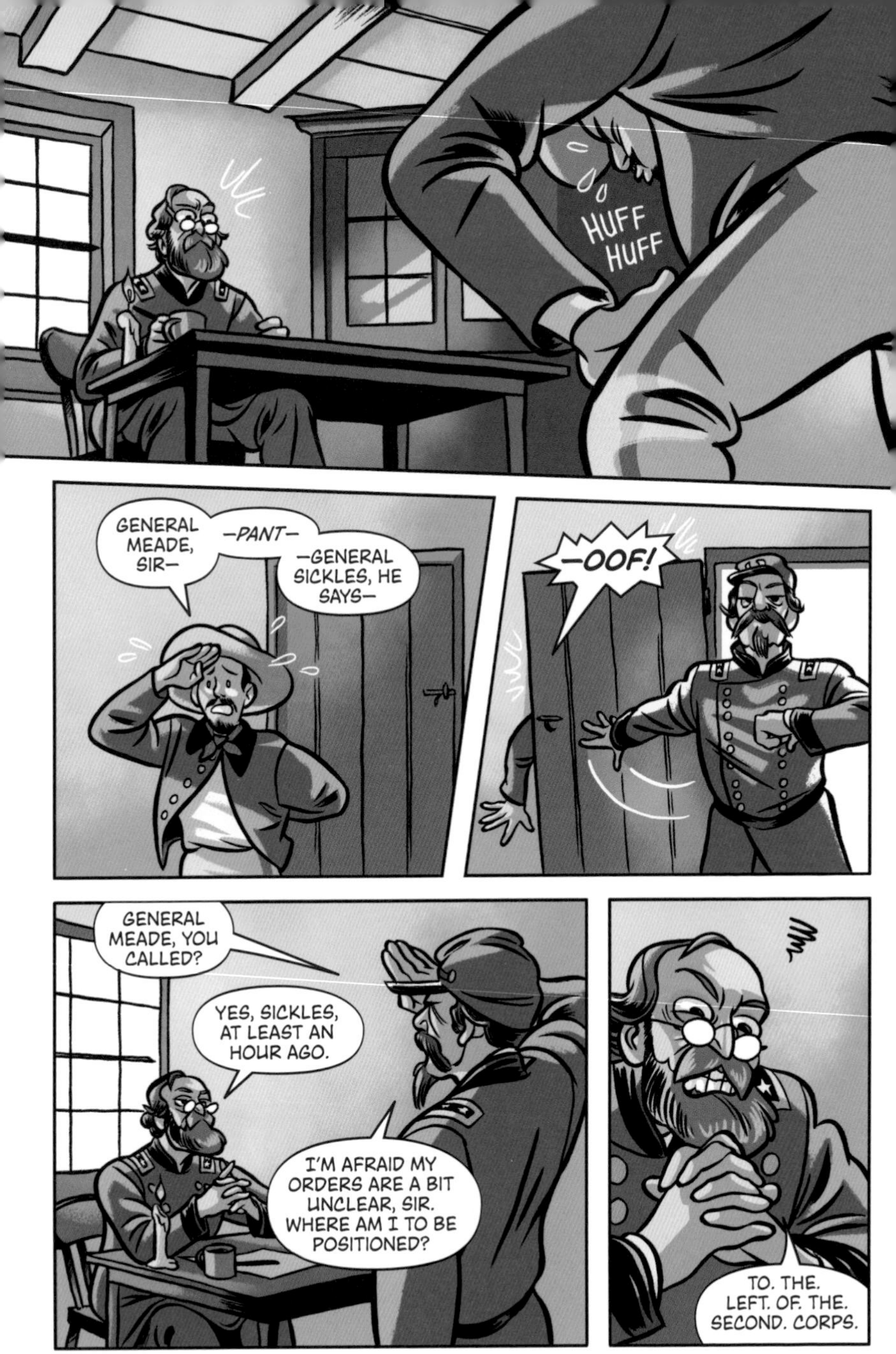
HUFF
HUFF
GENERAL MEADE, SIR—
—PANT—
—GENERAL SICKLES, HE SAYS—
—OOF!
GENERAL MEADE, YOU CALLED?
YES, SICKLES, AT LEAST AN HOUR AGO.
I'M AFRAID MY ORDERS ARE A BIT UNCLEAR, SIR. WHERE AM I TO BE POSITIONED?
TO. THE. LEFT. OF. THE. SECOND. CORPS.

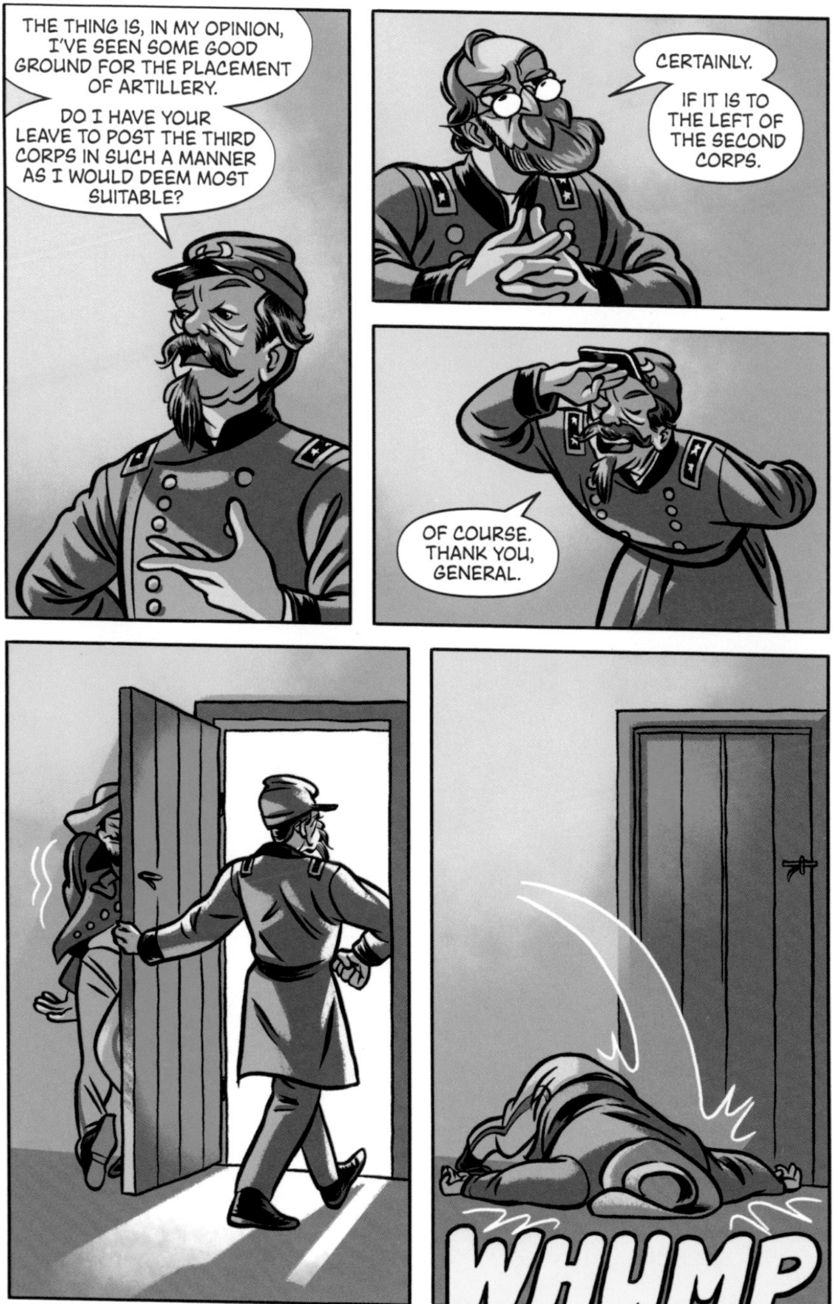
THE THING IS, IN MY OPINION, I'VE SEEN SOME GOOD GROUND FOR THE PLACEMENT OF ARTILLERY.
DO I HAVE YOUR LEAVE TO POST THE THIRD CORPS IN SUCH A MANNER AS I WOULD DEEM MOST SUITABLE?
CERTAINLY.
IF IT IS TO THE LEFT OF THE SECOND CORPS.
OF COURSE. THANK YOU, GENERAL.
WHUMP

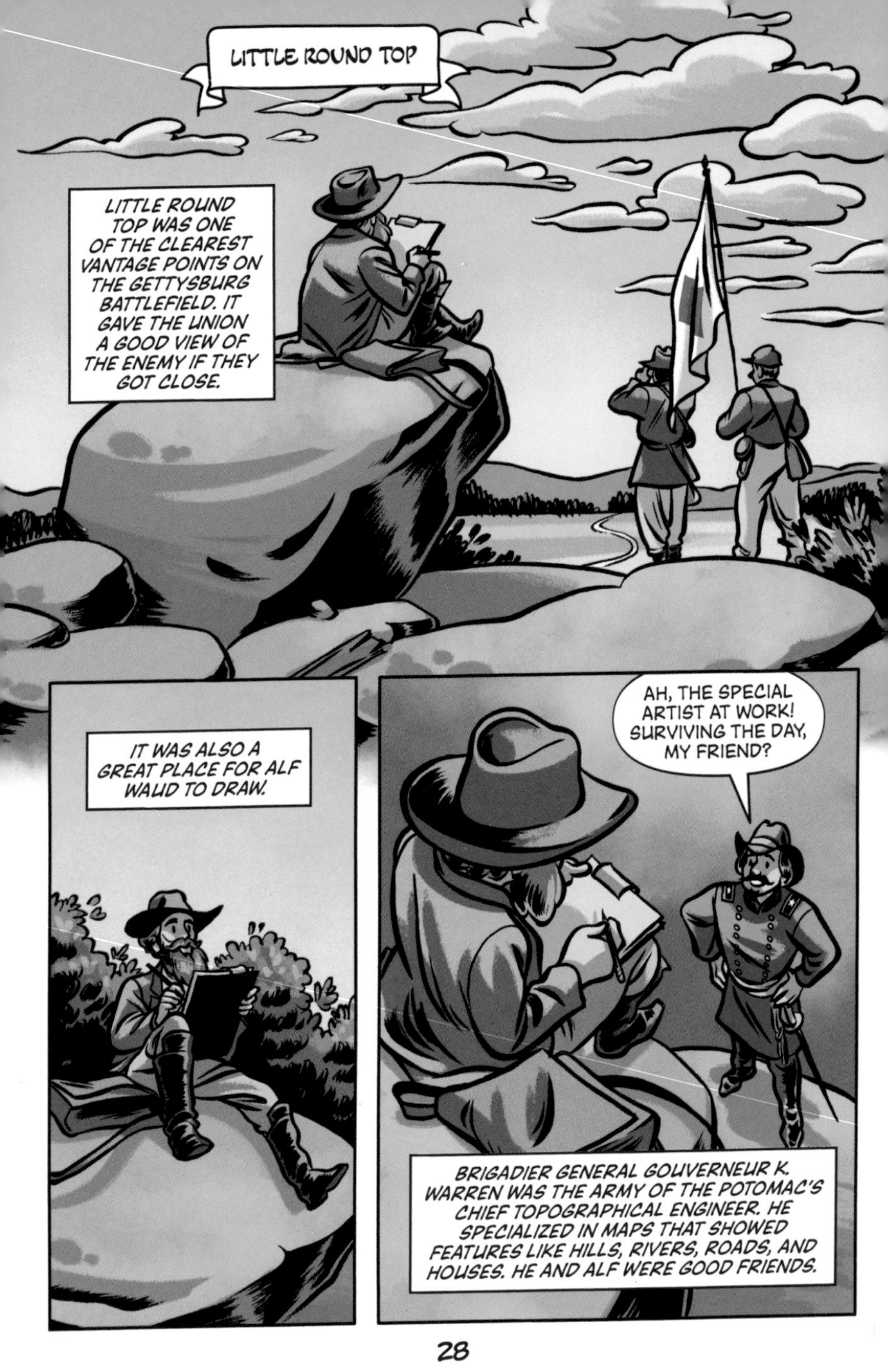
LITTLE ROUND TOP
LITTLE ROUND TOP WAS ONE OF THE CLEAREST VANTAGE POINTS ON THE GETTYSBURG BATTLEFIELD. IT GAVE THE UNION A GOOD VIEW OF THE ENEMY IF THEY GOT CLOSE.
IT WAS ALSO A GREAT PLACE FOR ALF WAUD TO DRAW.
AH, THE SPECIAL ARTIST AT WORK! SURVIVING THE DAY, MY FRIEND?
BRIGADIER GENERAL GOUVERNEUR K. WARREN WAS THE ARMY OF THE POTOMAC'S CHIEF TOPOGRAPHICAL ENGINEER. HE SPECIALIZED IN MAPS THAT SHOWED FEATURES LIKE HILLS, RIVERS, ROADS, AND HOUSES. HE AND ALF WERE GOOD FRIENDS.

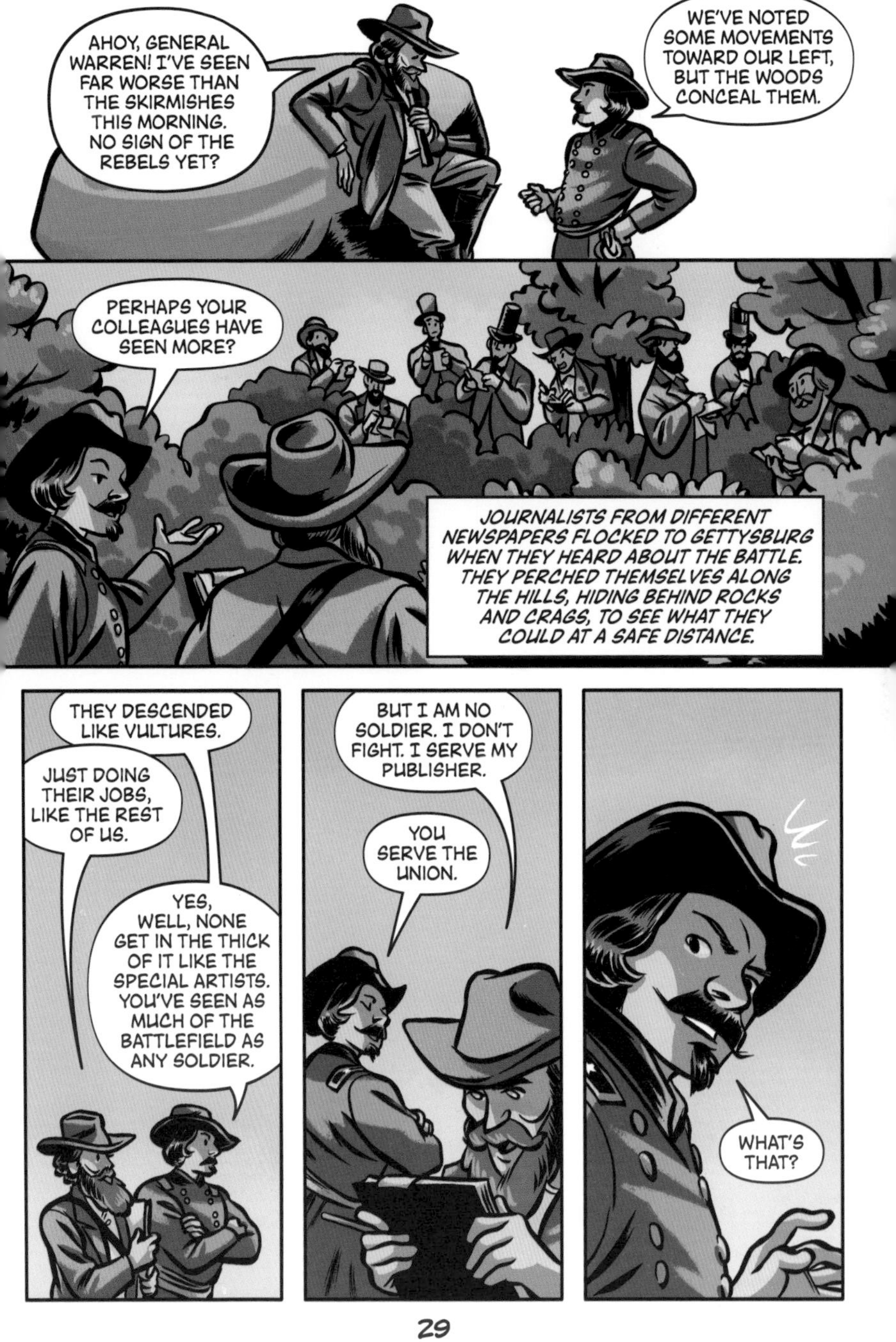
AHOY, GENERAL WARREN! I'VE SEEN FAR WORSE THAN THE SKIRMISHES THIS MORNING. NO SIGN OF THE REBELS YET?
WE'VE NOTED SOME MOVEMENTS TOWARD OUR LEFT, BUT THE WOODS CONCEAL THEM.
PERHAPS YOUR COLLEAGUES HAVE SEEN MORE?
JOURNALISTS FROM DIFFERENT NEWSPAPERS FLOCKED TO GETTYSBURG WHEN THEY HEARD ABOUT THE BATTLE. THEY PERCHED THEMSELVES ALONG THE HILLS, HIDING BEHIND ROCKS AND CRAGS, TO SEE WHAT THEY COULD AT A SAFE DISTANCE.
THEY DESCENDED LIKE VULTURES.
JUST DOING THEIR JOBS, LIKE THE REST OF US.
YES, WELL, NONE GET IN THE THICK OF IT LIKE THE SPECIAL ARTISTS. YOU'VE SEEN AS MUCH OF THE BATTLEFIELD AS ANY SOLDIER.
BUT I AM NO SOLDIER. I DON'T FIGHT. I SERVE MY PUBLISHER.
YOU SERVE THE UNION.
WHAT'S THAT?

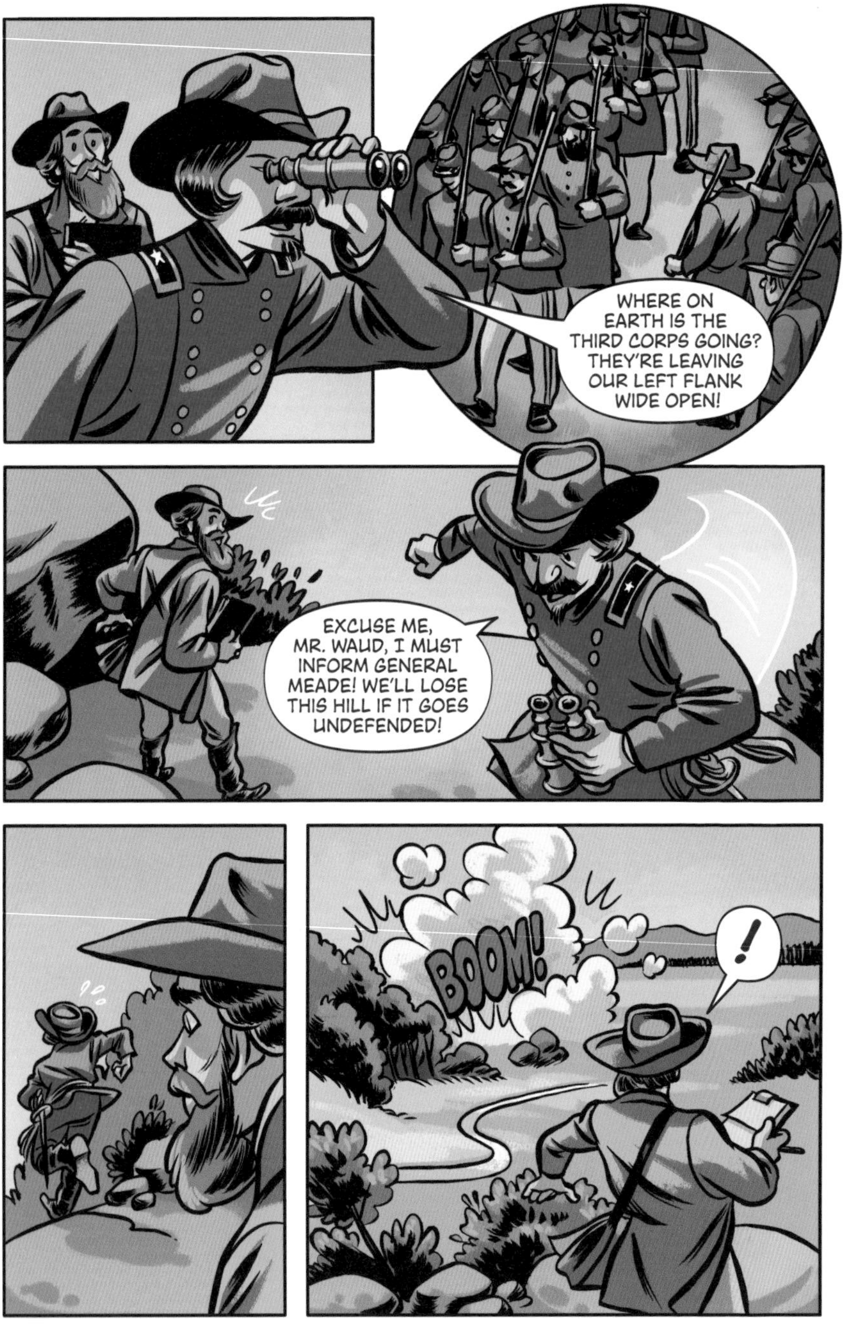
WHERE ON EARTH IS THE THIRD CORPS GOING? THEY'RE LEAVING OUR LEFT FLANK WIDE OPEN!
EXCUSE ME, MR. WAUD, I MUST INFORM GENERAL MEADE! WE'LL LOSE THIS HILL IF IT GOES UNDEFENDED!
BOOM!
!

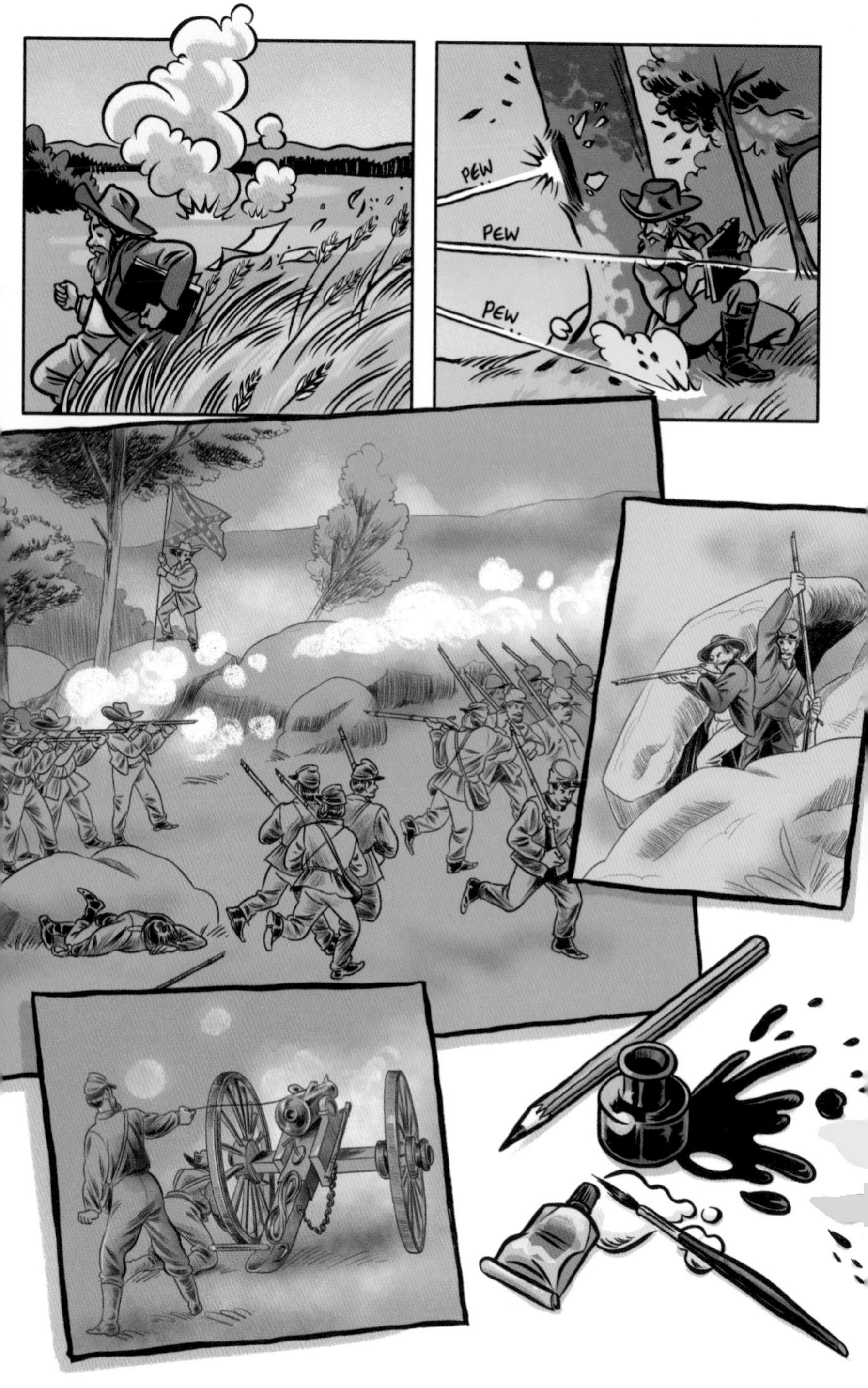
PEW
PEW
PEW

Devil's Den

On the second day of the Battle of Gettysburg, General Sickles saw an elevated plain between a peach orchard and a rocky area called Devil's Den, west of where Meade ordered him to place his Third Corps. He thought this would be a good spot for his artillery batteries (his cannons and gunmen). However, this was too far from the Second Corps at Cemetery Ridge. It exposed the left side of the Union army to attack and left Little Round Top open for capture. Sickles moved his men anyway.

Meanwhile, Confederate general James Longstreet was preparing his troops for an attack. Completely by accident, Sickles placed his Third Corps directly in Longstreet's way. The Confederates weren't expecting to find Union forces there at all.

The Confederate troops attacked. General Meade sent reinforcements, but the Third Corps was too far out of range for much help. Both armies suffered terrible losses, Sickles's men most of all. Union troops had to retreat. General Sickles lost his right leg in the battle and would not fight again for the rest of the Civil War.

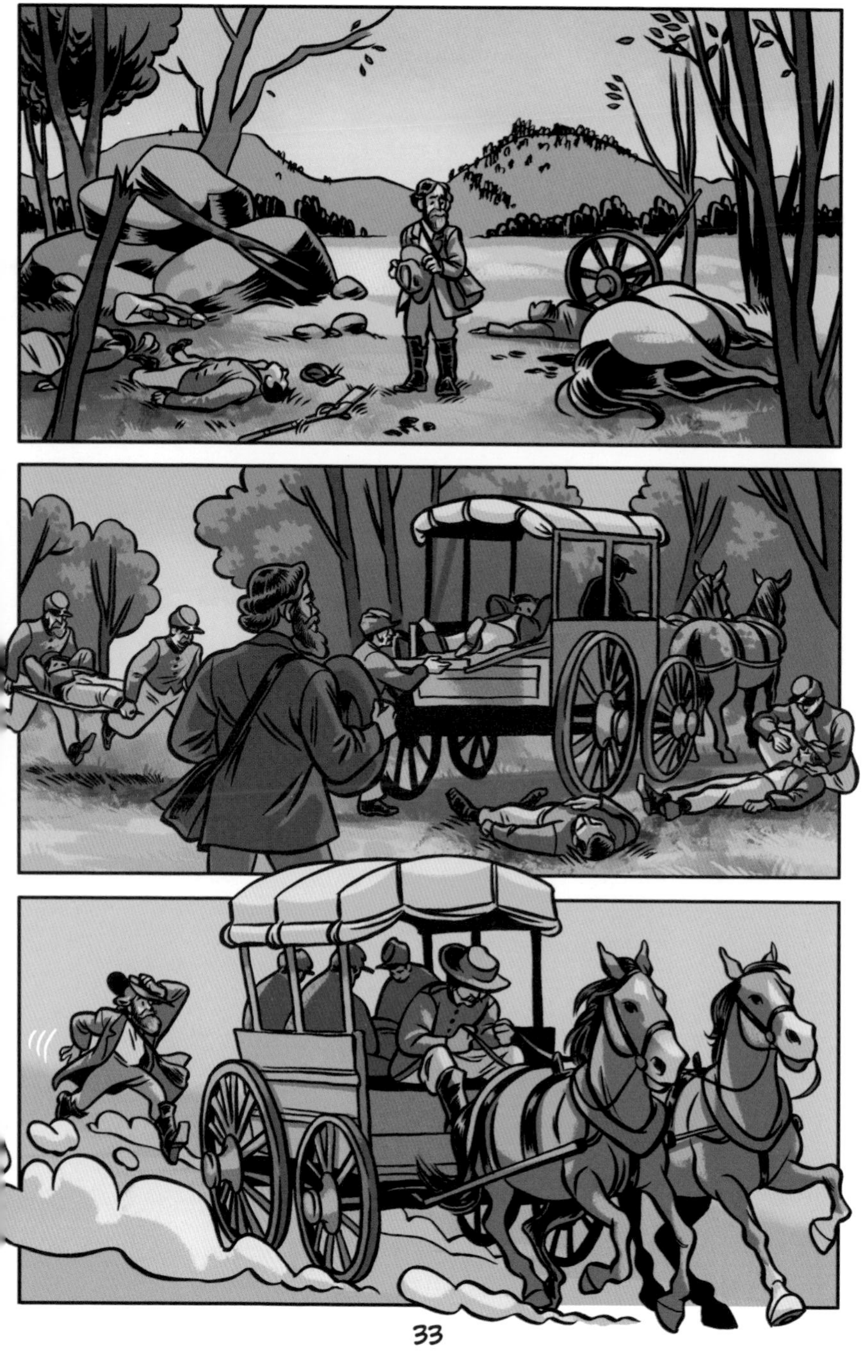

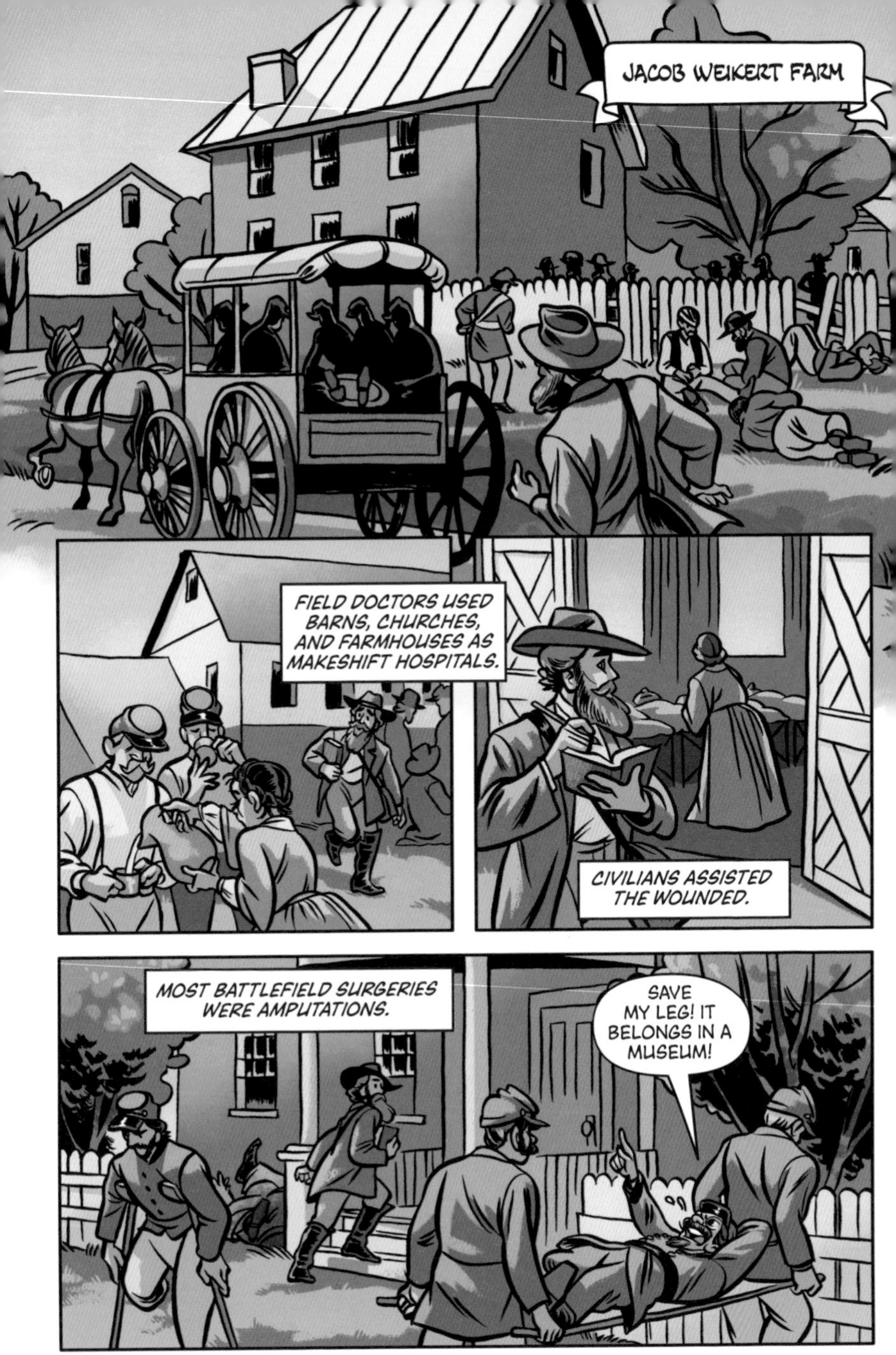
JACOB WEIKERT FARM
FIELD DOCTORS USED BARNS, CHURCHES, AND FARMHOUSES AS MAKESHIFT HOSPITALS.
CIVILIANS ASSISTED THE WOUNDED.
MOST BATTLEFIELD SURGERIES WERE AMPUTATIONS.
SAVE MY LEG! IT BELONGS IN A MUSEUM!

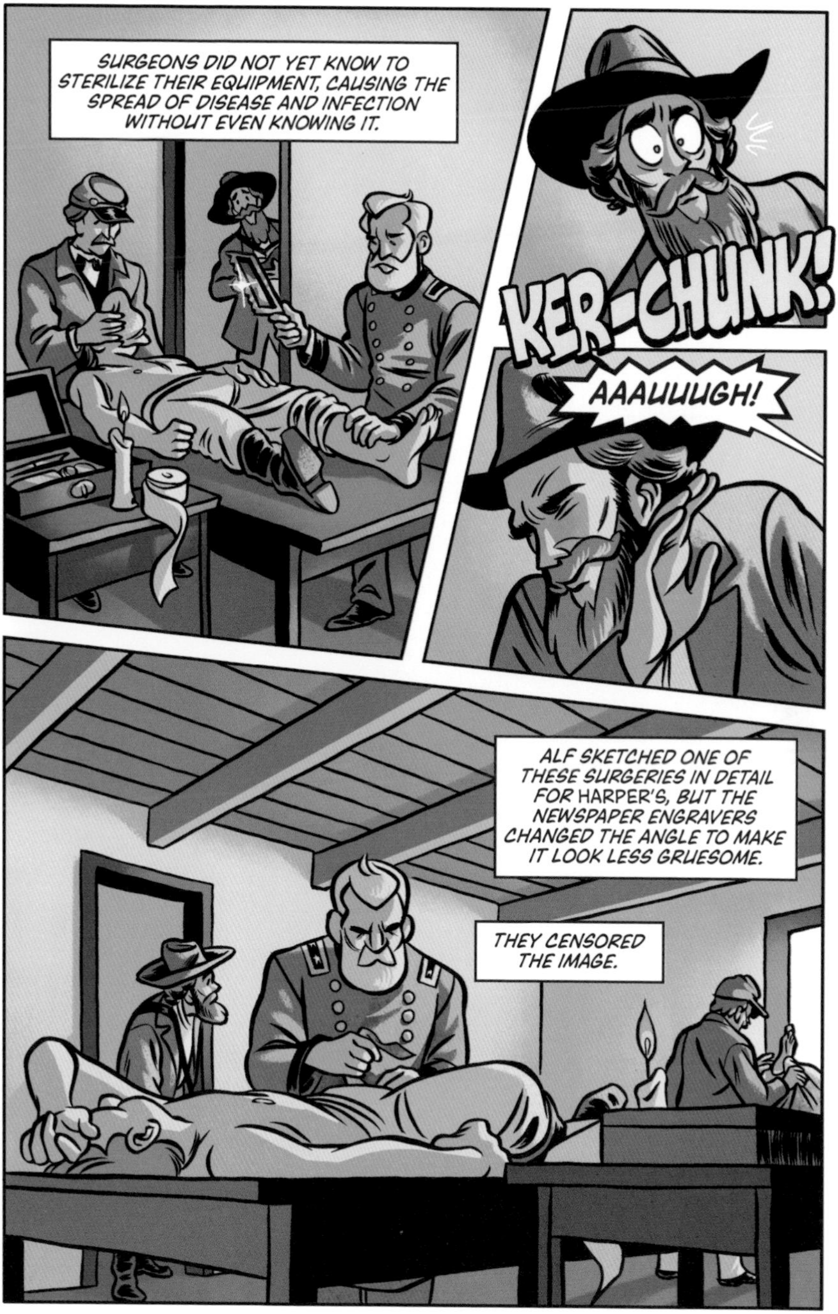
SURGEONS DID NOT YET KNOW TO STERILIZE THEIR EQUIPMENT, CAUSING THE SPREAD OF DISEASE AND INFECTION WITHOUT EVEN KNOWING IT.
KER-CHUNK!
AAAUUUGH!
ALF SKETCHED ONE OF THESE SURGERIES IN DETAIL FOR HARPER'S, BUT THE NEWSPAPER ENGRAVERS CHANGED THE ANGLE TO MAKE IT LOOK LESS GRUESOME.
THEY CENSORED THE IMAGE.

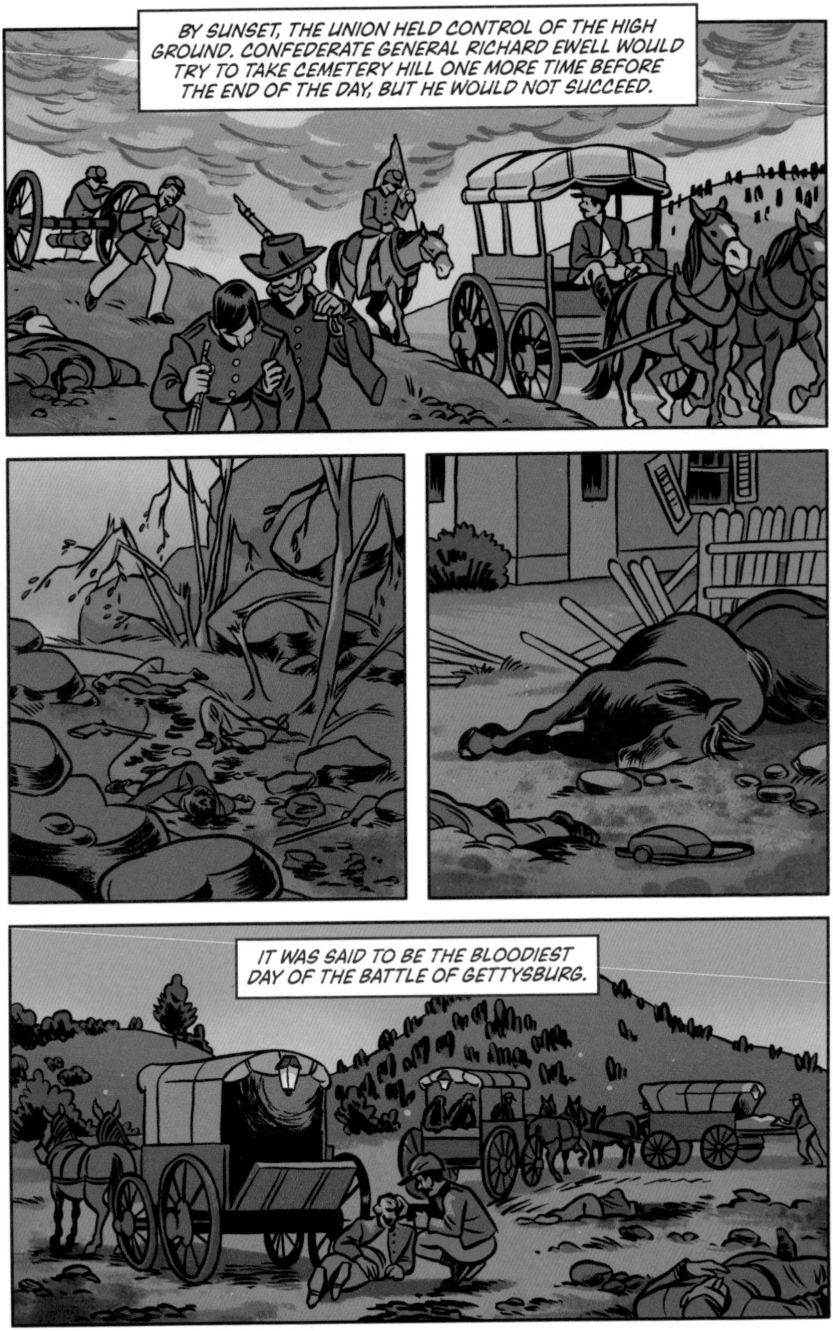
BY SUNSET, THE UNION HELD CONTROL OF THE HIGH GROUND. CONFEDERATE GENERAL RICHARD EWELL WOULD TRY TO TAKE CEMETERY HILL ONE MORE TIME BEFORE THE END OF THE DAY, BUT HE WOULD NOT SUCCEED.
IT WAS SAID TO BE THE BLOODIEST DAY OF THE BATTLE OF GETTYSBURG.

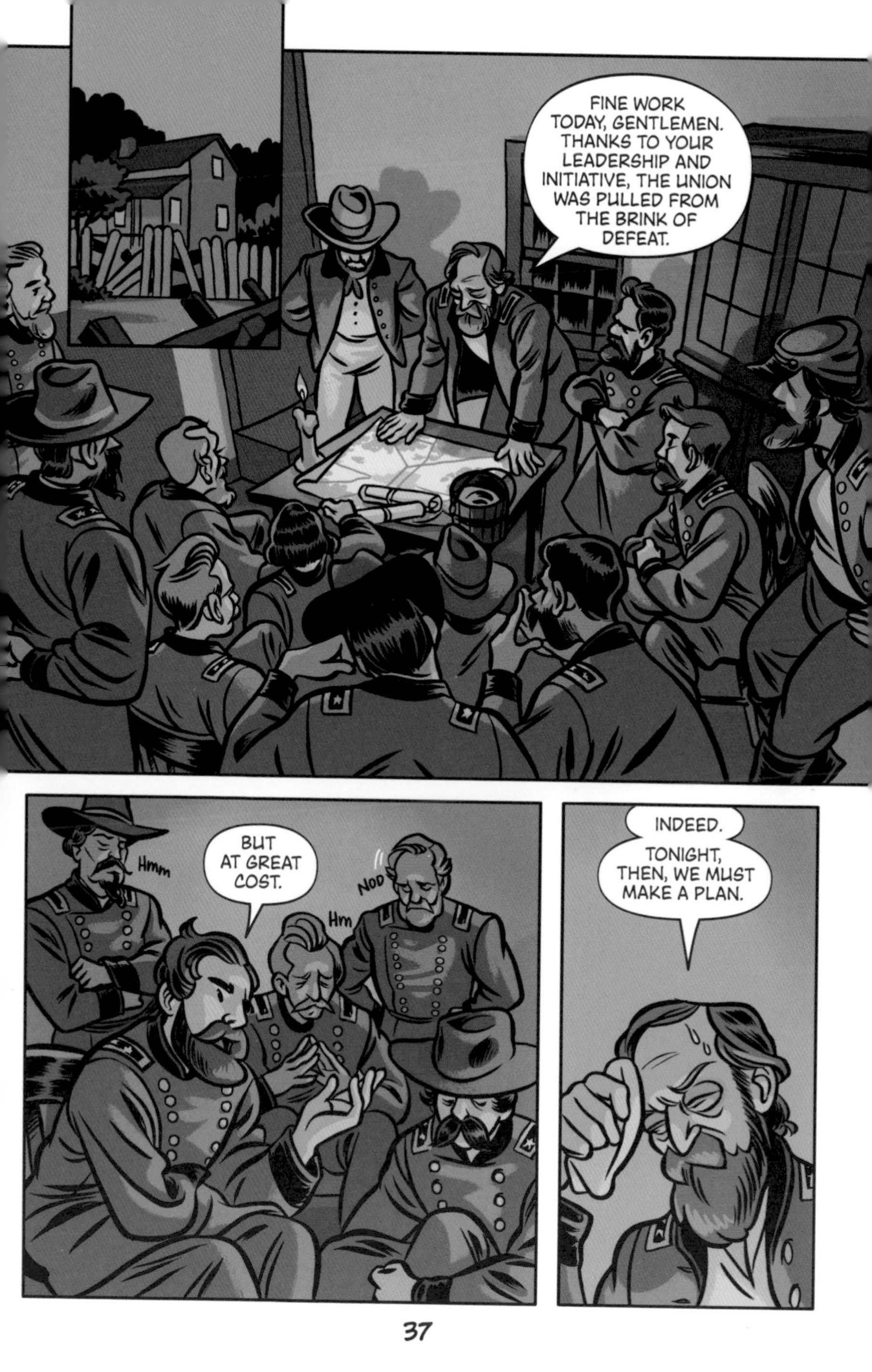
FINE WORK TODAY, GENTLEMEN. THANKS TO YOUR LEADERSHIP AND INITIATIVE, THE UNION WAS PULLED FROM THE BRINK OF DEFEAT.
Hmm
BUT AT GREAT COST.
NOD
Hm
INDEED.
TONIGHT, THEN, WE MUST MAKE A PLAN.

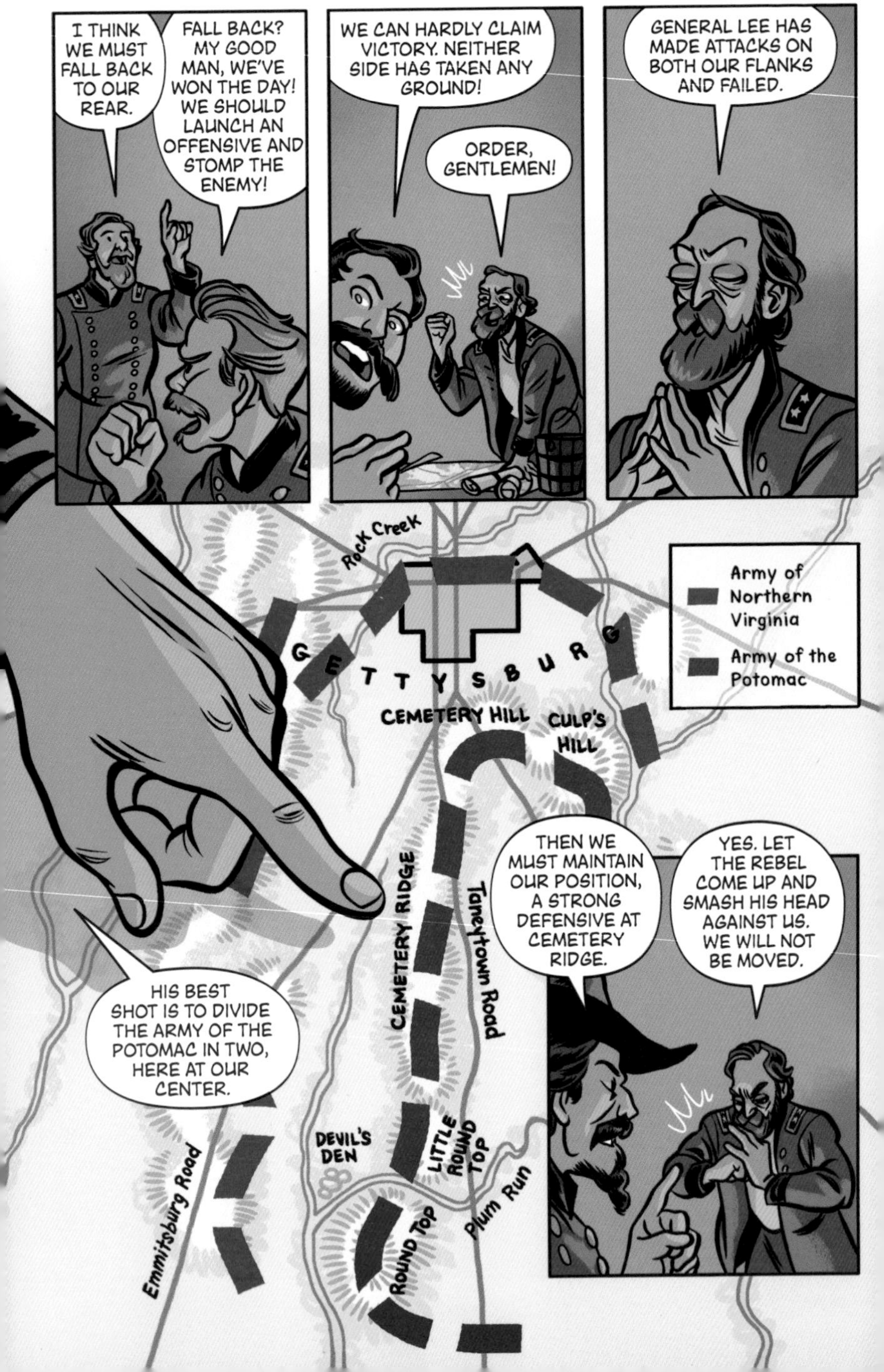
I THINK WE MUST FALL BACK TO OUR REAR.
FALL BACK? MY GOOD MAN, WE'VE WON THE DAY! WE SHOULD LAUNCH AN OFFENSIVE AND STOMP THE ENEMY!
WE CAN HARDLY CLAIM VICTORY. NEITHER SIDE HAS TAKEN ANY GROUND!
ORDER, GENTLEMEN!
GENERAL LEE HAS MADE ATTACKS ON BOTH OUR FLANKS AND FAILED.
Rock Creek
GETTYSBURG
Army of Northern Virginia
Army of the Potomac
CEMETERY HILL
CULP'S HILL
CEMETERY RIDGE
Taneytown Road
HIS BEST SHOT IS TO DIVIDE THE ARMY OF THE POTOMAC IN TWO, HERE AT OUR CENTER.
THEN WE MUST MAINTAIN OUR POSITION, A STRONG DEFENSIVE AT CEMETERY RIDGE.
YES. LET THE REBEL COME UP AND SMASH HIS HEAD AGAINST US. WE WILL NOT BE MOVED.
DEVIL'S DEN
LITTLE ROUND TOP
Emmitsburg Road
ROUND TOP
Plum Run

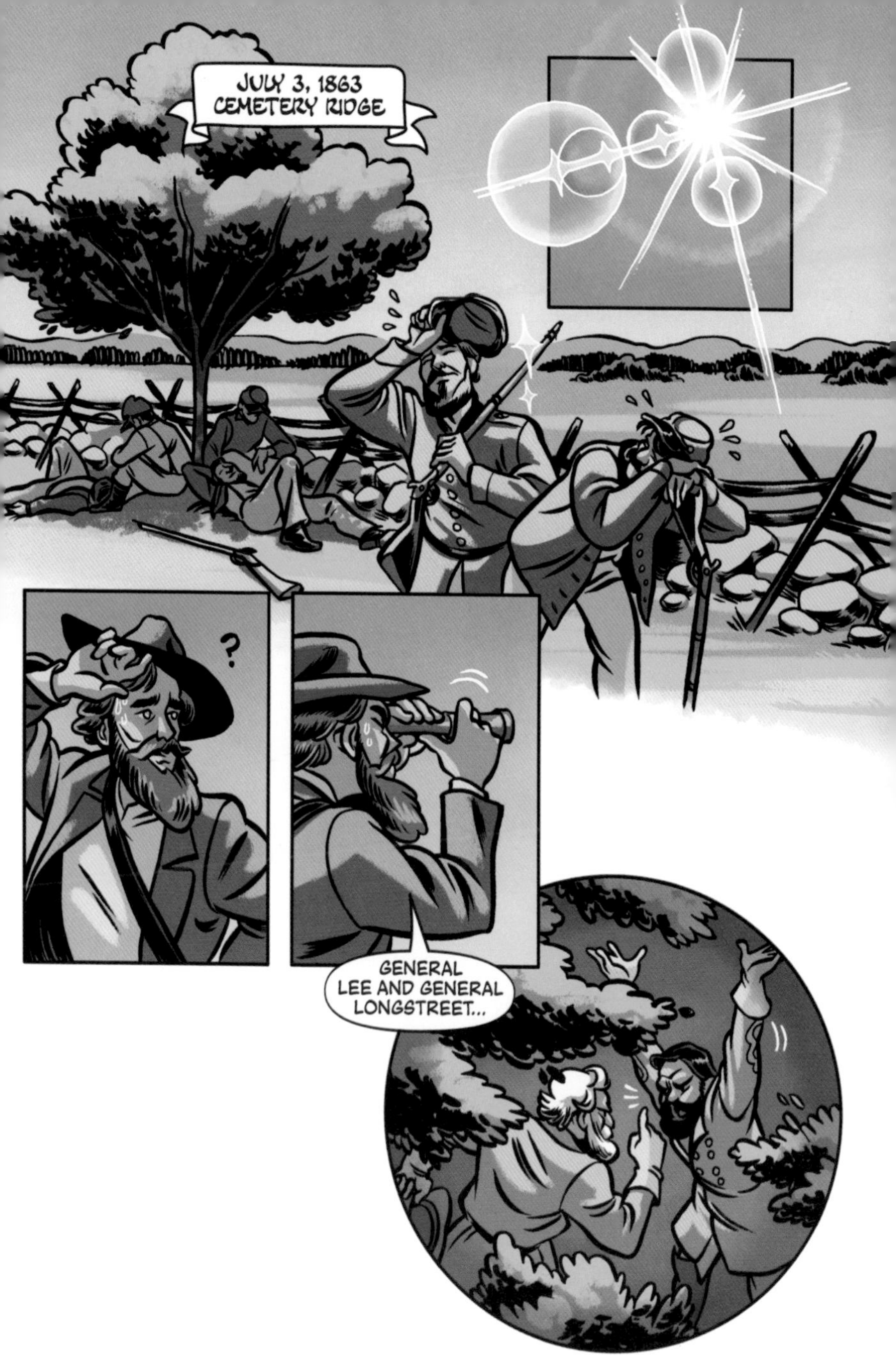
JULY 3, 1863
CEMETERY RIDGE
?
GENERAL LEE AND GENERAL LONGSTREET...

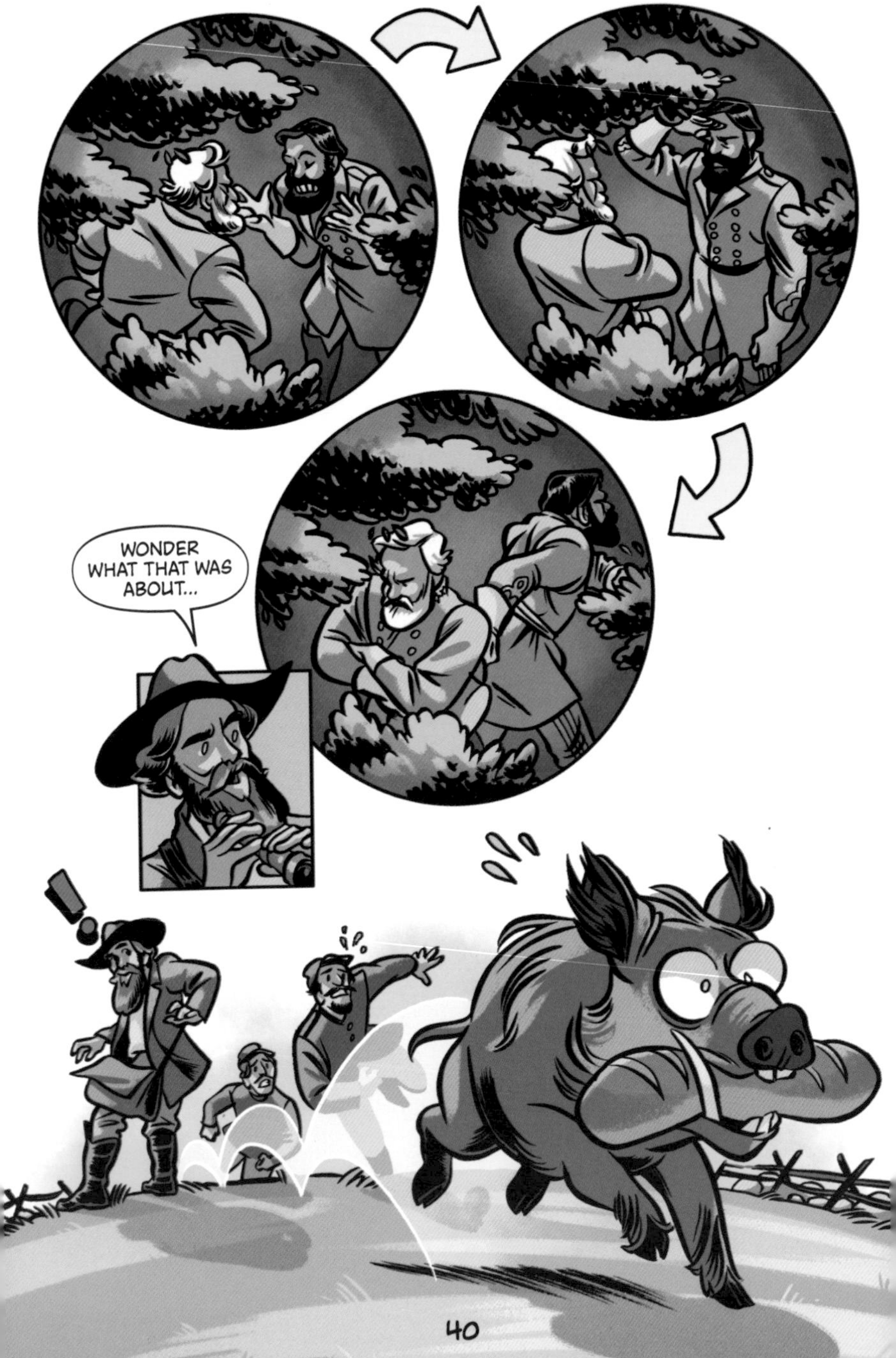
WONDER WHAT THAT WAS ABOUT...

General James Longstreet

General James Longstreet was leader of the Confederate army's First Corps and one of General Lee's best officers. Lee affectionately called him "my old war horse." Longstreet, however, clashed with Lee on many decisions made at Gettysburg. Longstreet didn't want to fight at Gettysburg at all—his hope was to form a strong defensive elsewhere, forcing the Union to initiate battle on Confederate terms. But Lee's "blood was up," as Longstreet put it, and he would not change course.

Longstreet commanded General George Pickett's division. On July 3, 1863, he reluctantly made the order for what would be known as Pickett's Charge. Longstreet said, "Never was I so depressed as on that day. I felt my men were to be sacrificed, and that I should have to order them to make a helpless charge."

After the Civil War, Longstreet publicly spoke about his disapproval of Lee's tactics and later became a supporter of Lincoln's Republican party. A group of former Confederates called the "Lee cult" would not stand for any criticism of their general and called Longstreet a traitor. Longstreet spent the rest of his life defending himself against Lee supporters.

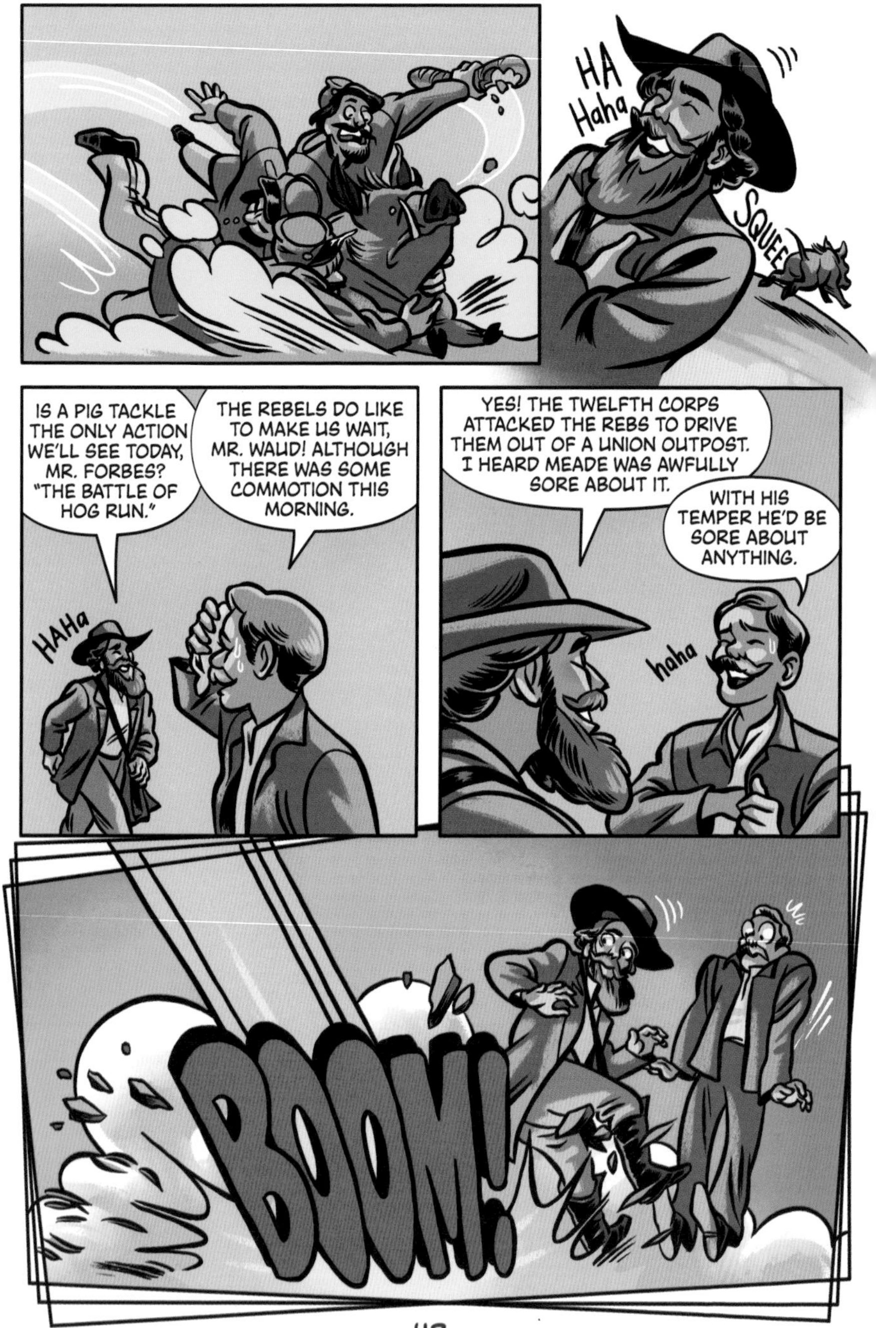
HA
Haha
SQUEE
IS A PIG TACKLE THE ONLY ACTION WE'LL SEE TODAY, MR. FORBES? "THE BATTLE OF HOG RUN."
THE REBELS DO LIKE TO MAKE US WAIT, MR. WAUD! ALTHOUGH THERE WAS SOME COMMOTION THIS MORNING.
HAHa
YES! THE TWELFTH CORPS ATTACKED THE REBS TO DRIVE THEM OUT OF A UNION OUTPOST. I HEARD MEADE WAS AWFULLY SORE ABOUT IT.
WITH HIS TEMPER HE'D BE SORE ABOUT ANYTHING.
haha
BOOM!

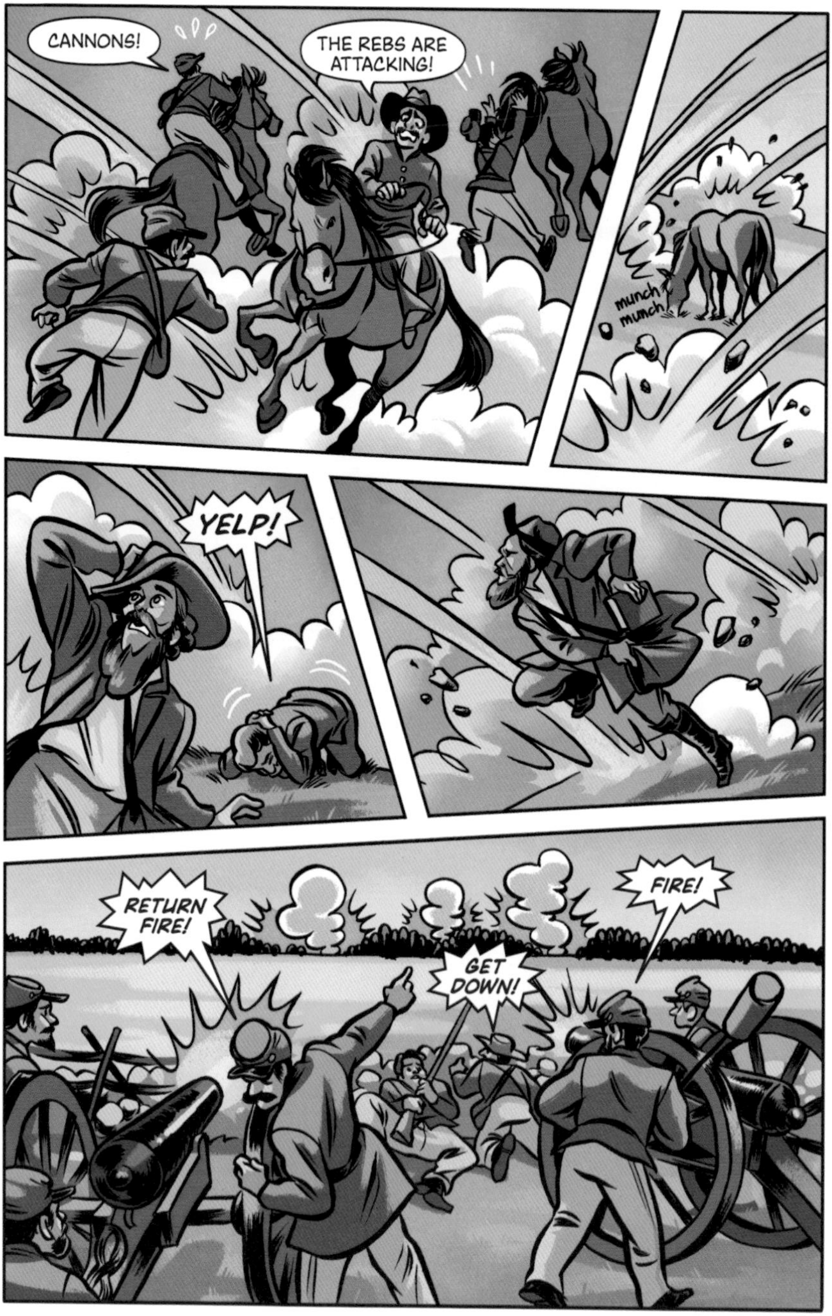
CANNONS!
THE REBS ARE ATTACKING!
munch munch
YELP!
RETURN FIRE!
GET DOWN!
FIRE!

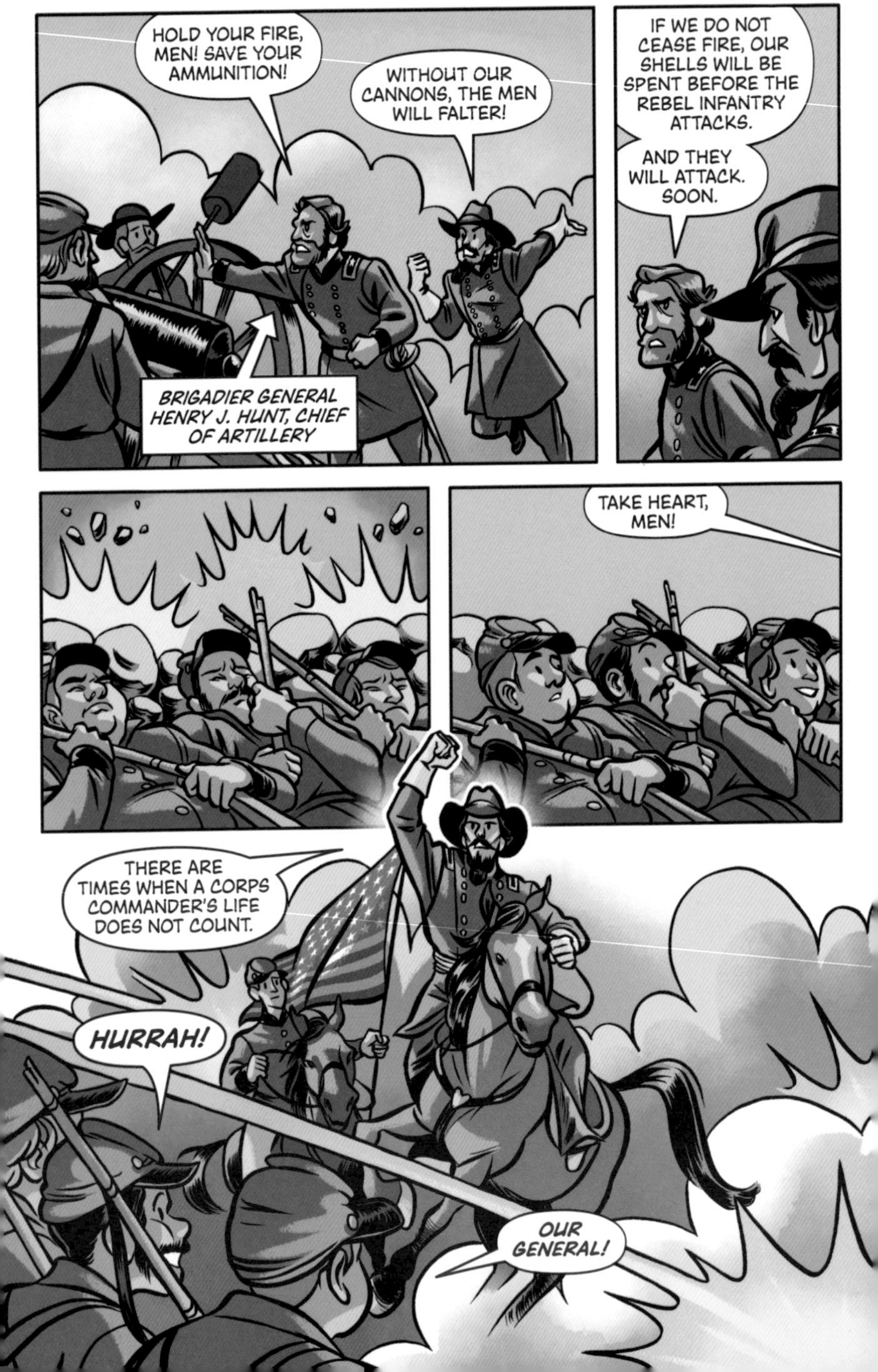
HOLD YOUR FIRE, MEN! SAVE YOUR AMMUNITION!
WITHOUT OUR CANNONS, THE MEN WILL FALTER!
BRIGADIER GENERAL HENRY J. HUNT, CHIEF OF ARTILLERY
IF WE DO NOT CEASE FIRE, OUR SHELLS WILL BE SPENT BEFORE THE REBEL INFANTRY ATTACKS.
AND THEY WILL ATTACK. SOON.
TAKE HEART, MEN!
THERE ARE TIMES WHEN A CORPS COMMANDER'S LIFE DOES NOT COUNT.
HURRAH!
OUR GENERAL!

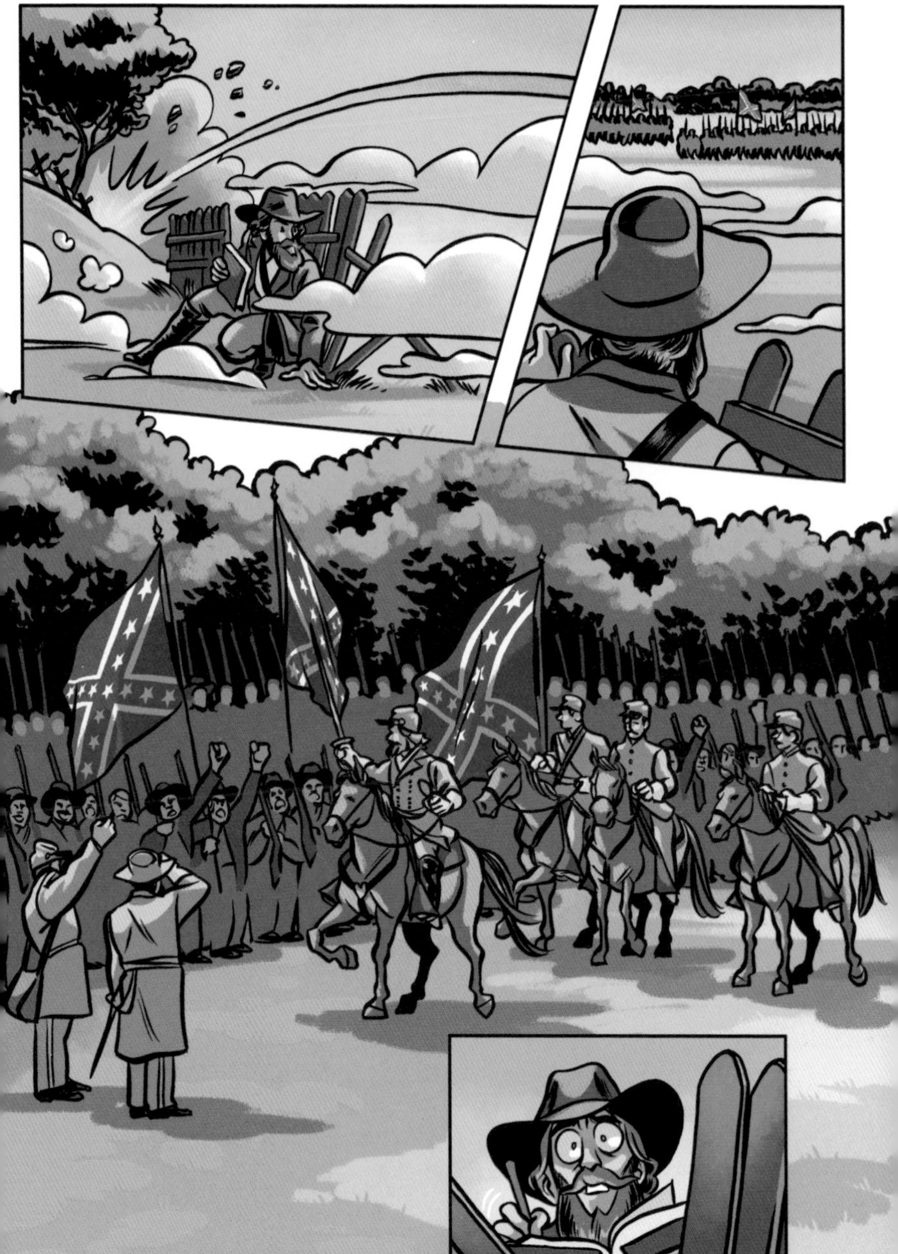

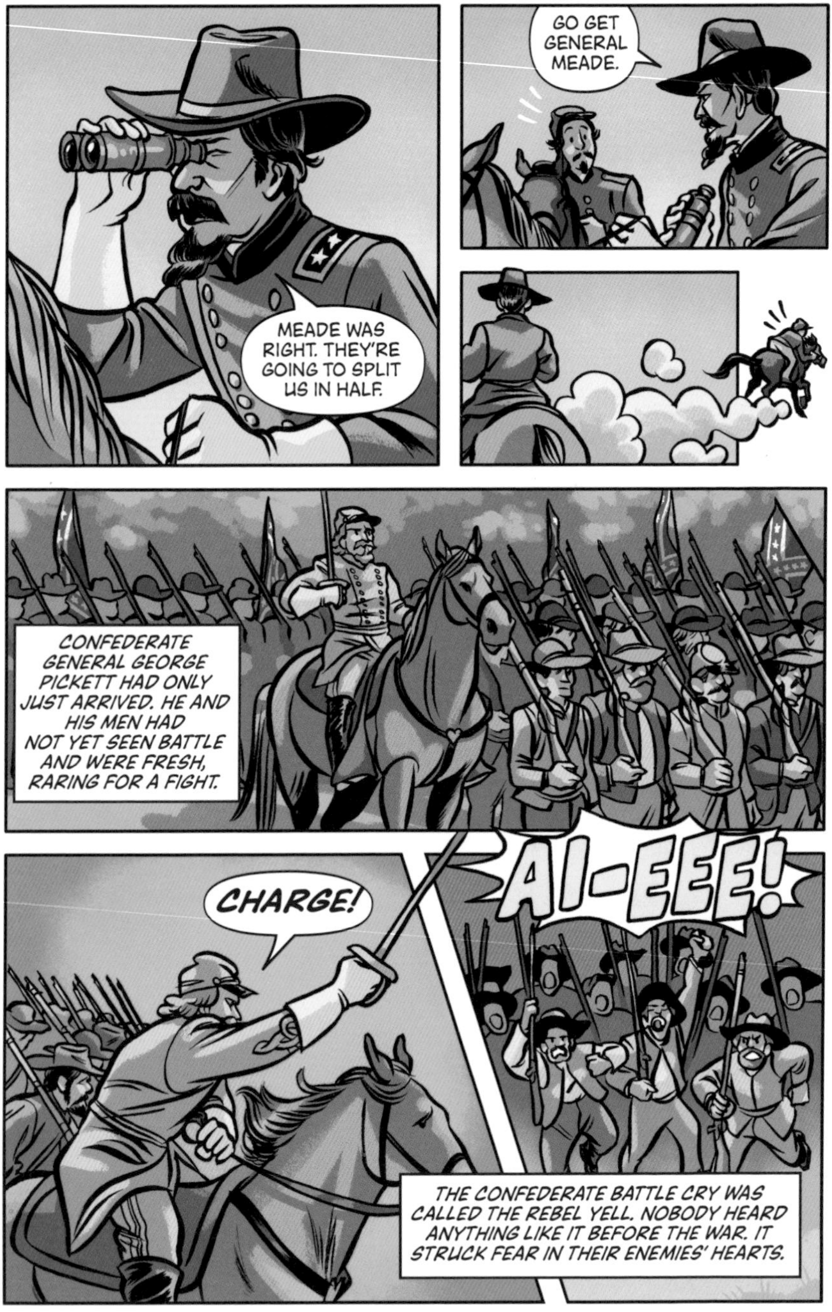
GO GET GENERAL MEADE.
MEADE WAS RIGHT. THEY'RE GOING TO SPLIT US IN HALF.
CONFEDERATE GENERAL GEORGE PICKETT HAD ONLY JUST ARRIVED. HE AND HIS MEN HAD NOT YET SEEN BATTLE AND WERE FRESH, RARING FOR A FIGHT.
CHARGE!
AI-EEE!
THE CONFEDERATE BATTLE CRY WAS CALLED THE REBEL YELL. NOBODY HEARD ANYTHING LIKE IT BEFORE THE WAR. IT STRUCK FEAR IN THEIR ENEMIES' HEARTS.

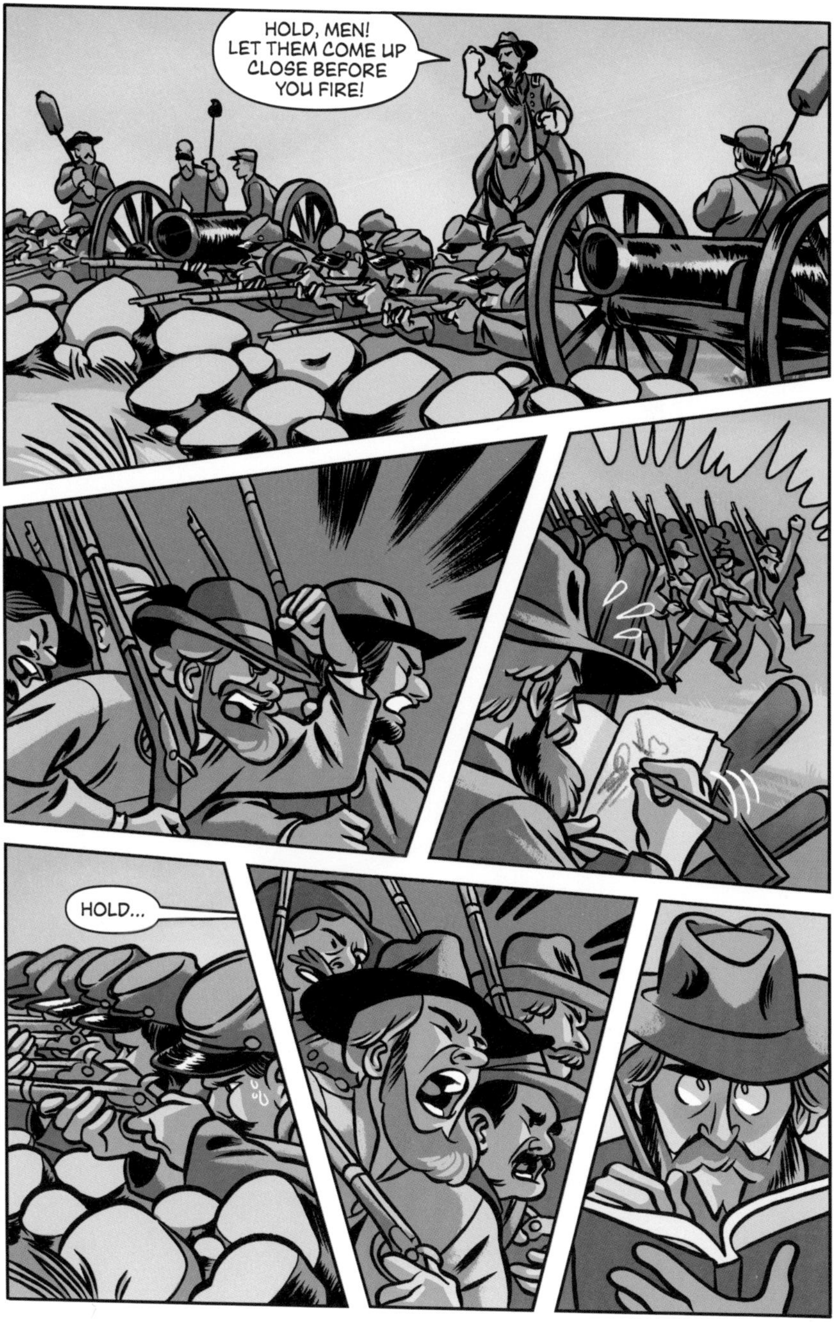
HOLD, MEN! LET THEM COME UP CLOSE BEFORE YOU FIRE!
HOLD...

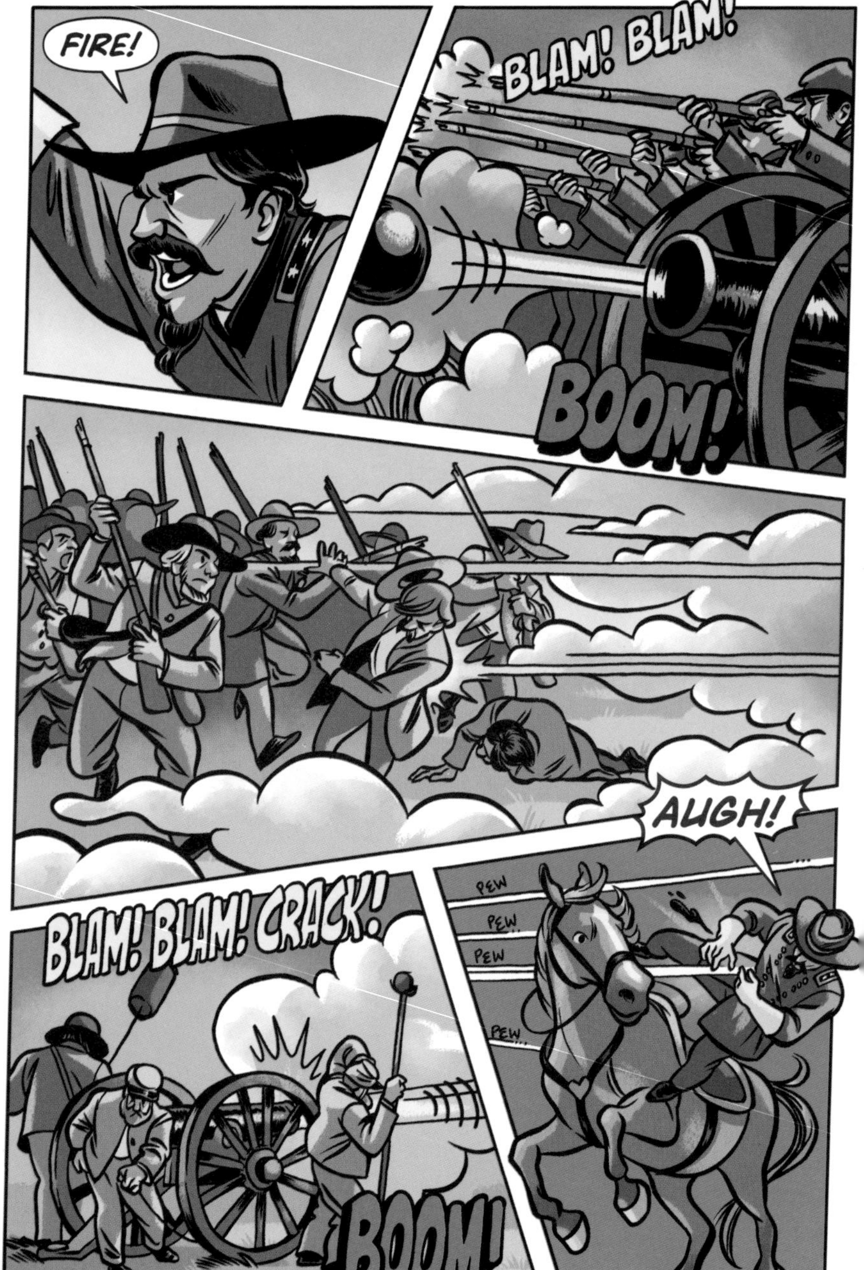
FIRE!
BLAM! BLAM!
BOOM!
AUGH!
PEW
PEW
PEW
PEW
BLAM! BLAM! CRACK!
BOOM!

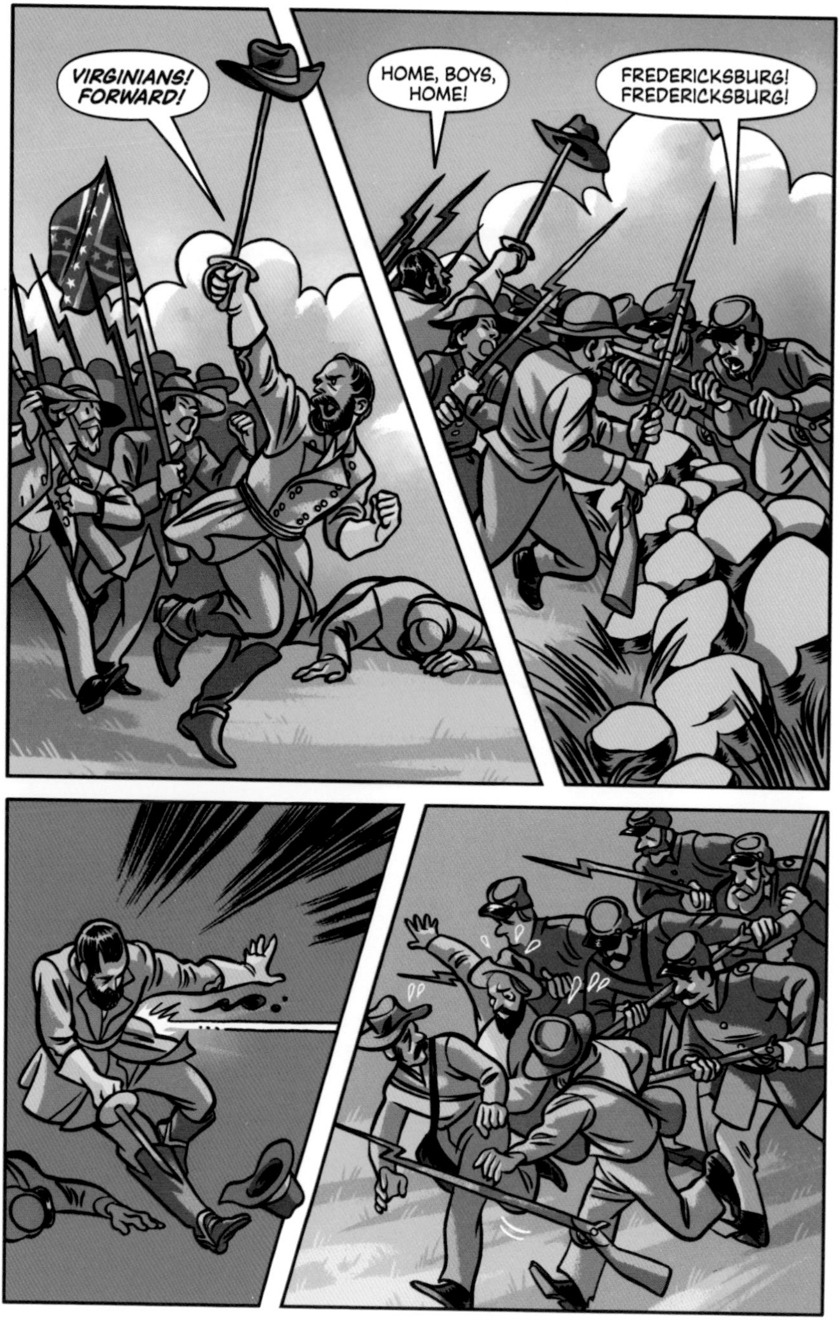
VIRGINIANS! FORWARD!
HOME, BOYS, HOME!
FREDERICKSBURG! FREDERICKSBURG!

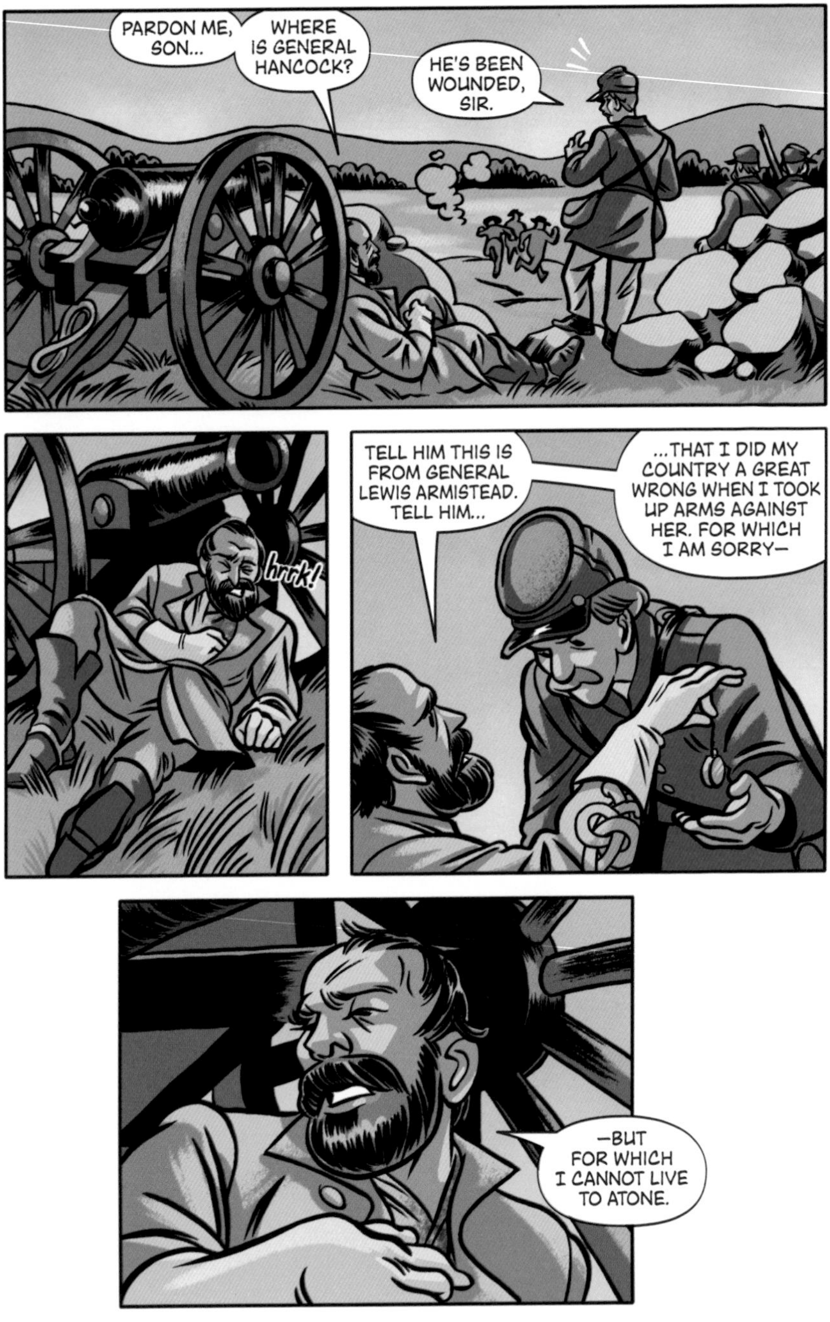
PARDON ME, SON...
WHERE IS GENERAL HANCOCK?
HE'S BEEN WOUNDED, SIR.
hrrk!
TELL HIM THIS IS FROM GENERAL LEWIS ARMISTEAD. TELL HIM...
...THAT I DID MY COUNTRY A GREAT WRONG WHEN I TOOK UP ARMS AGAINST HER. FOR WHICH I AM SORRY—
—BUT FOR WHICH I CANNOT LIVE TO ATONE.

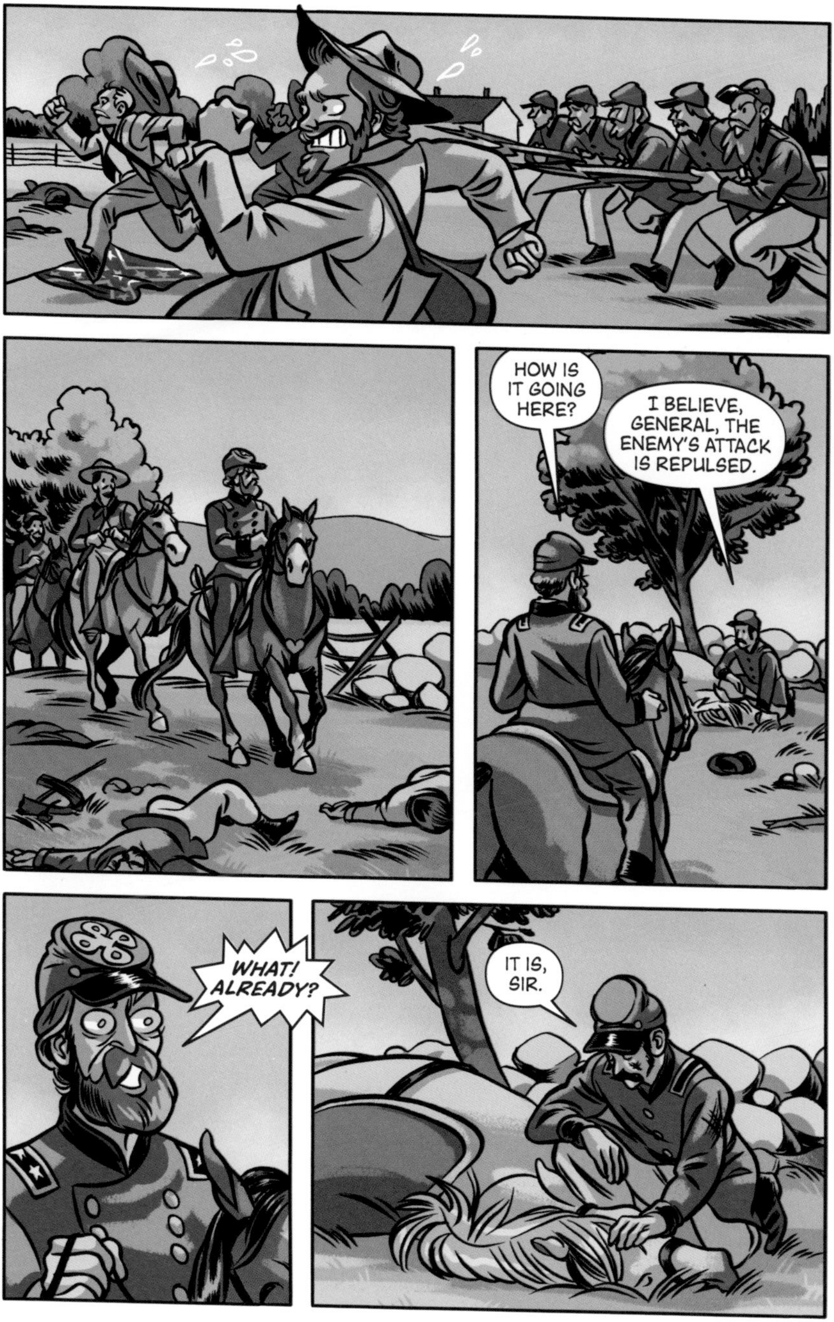
HOW IS
IT GOING
HERE?
I BELIEVE,
GENERAL, THE
ENEMY'S ATTACK
IS REPULSED.
WHAT!
ALREADY?
IT IS,
SIR.

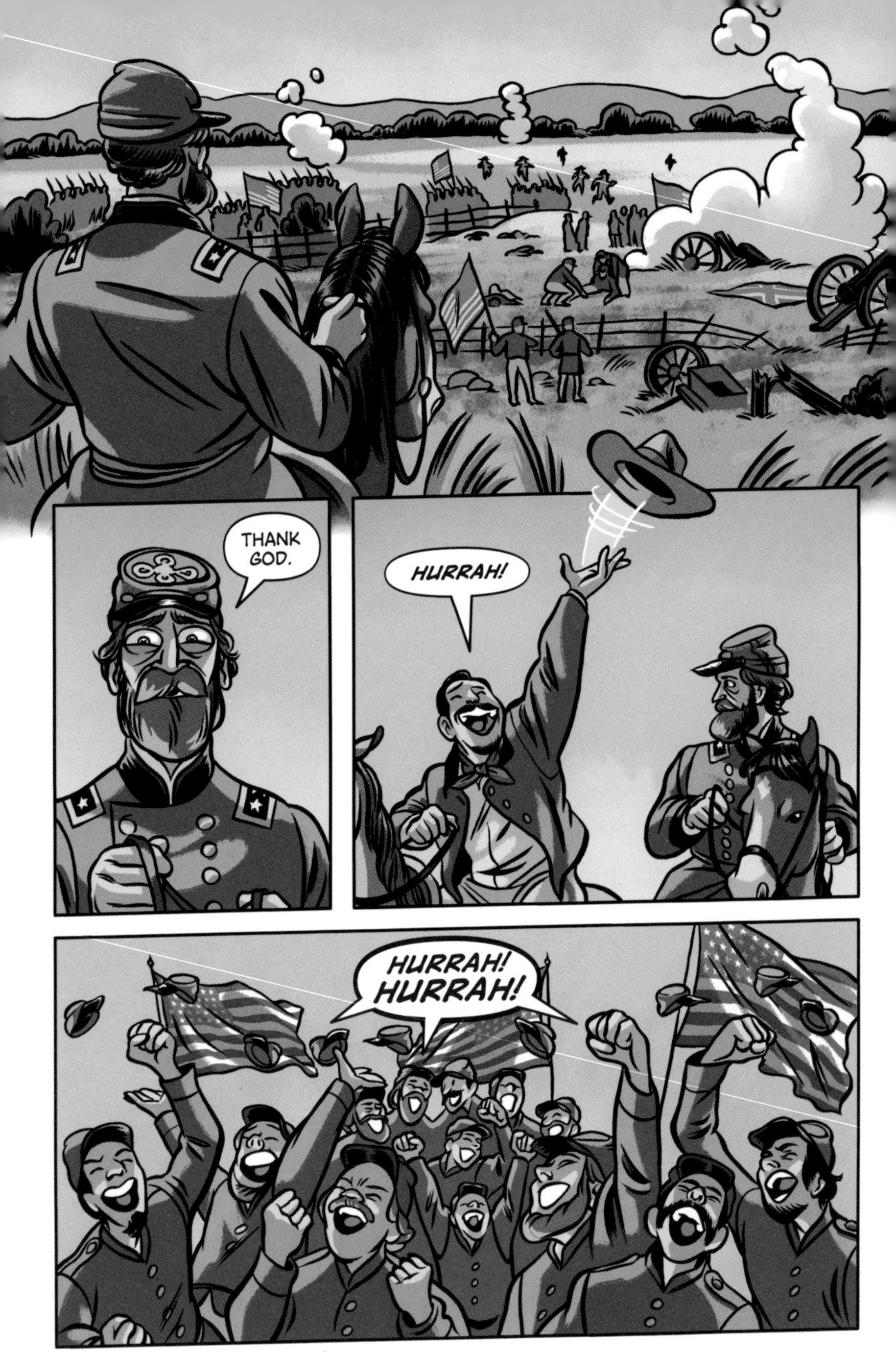
THANK GOD.
HURRAH!
HURRAH! HURRAH!

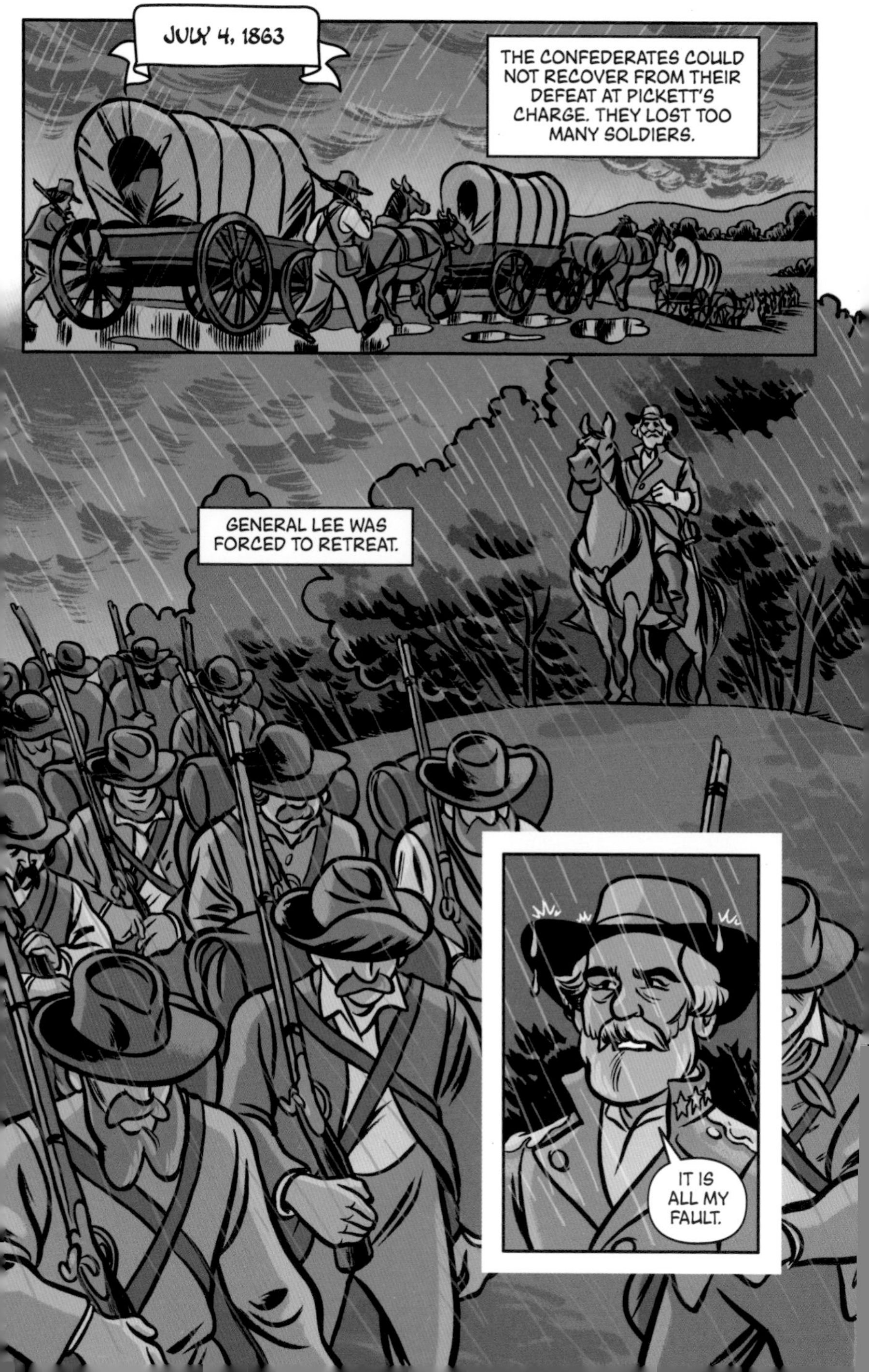
JULY 4, 1863
THE CONFEDERATES COULD NOT RECOVER FROM THEIR DEFEAT AT PICKETT'S CHARGE. THEY LOST TOO MANY SOLDIERS.
GENERAL LEE WAS FORCED TO RETREAT.
IT IS ALL MY FAULT.

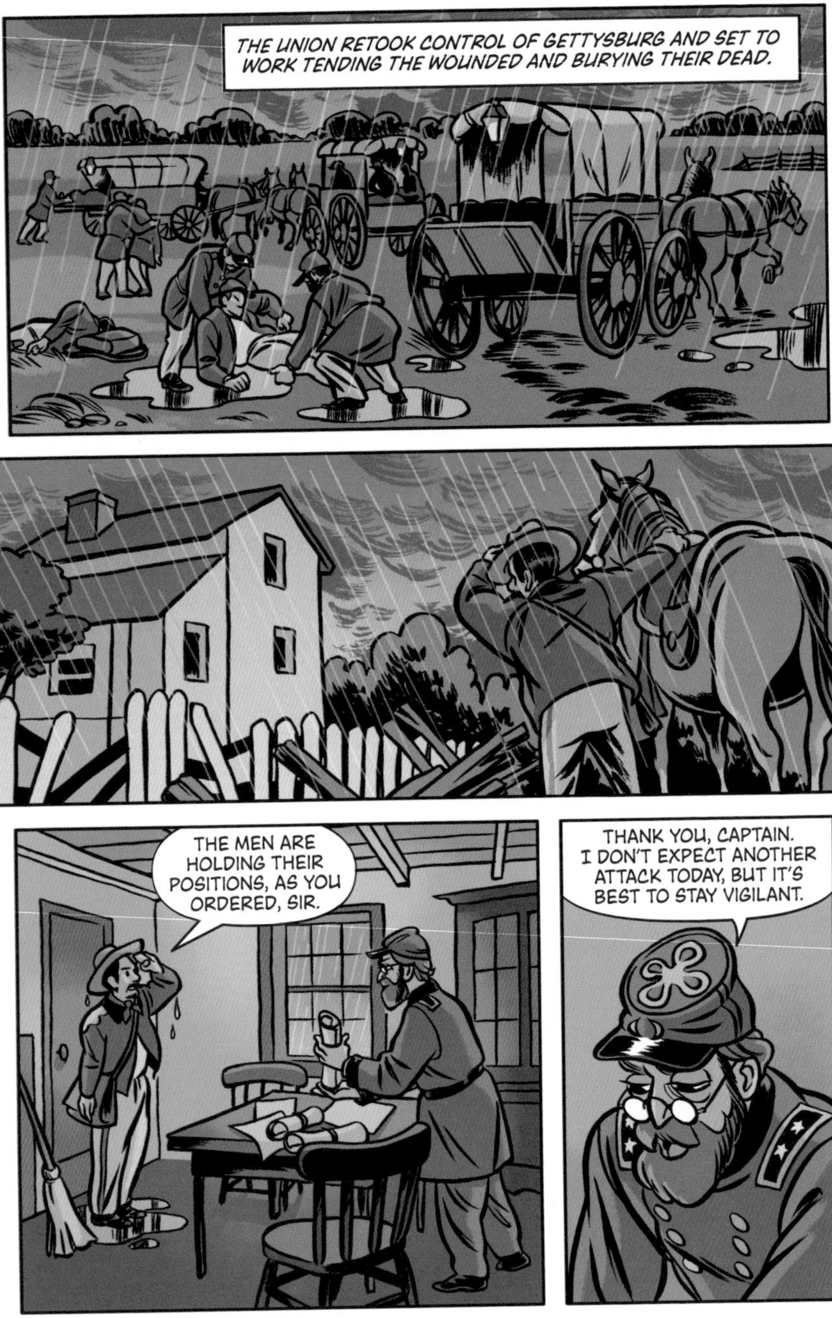
THE UNION RETOOK CONTROL OF GETTYSBURG AND SET TO WORK TENDING THE WOUNDED AND BURYING THEIR DEAD.
THE MEN ARE HOLDING THEIR POSITIONS, AS YOU ORDERED, SIR.
THANK YOU, CAPTAIN. I DON'T EXPECT ANOTHER ATTACK TODAY, BUT IT'S BEST TO STAY VIGILANT.

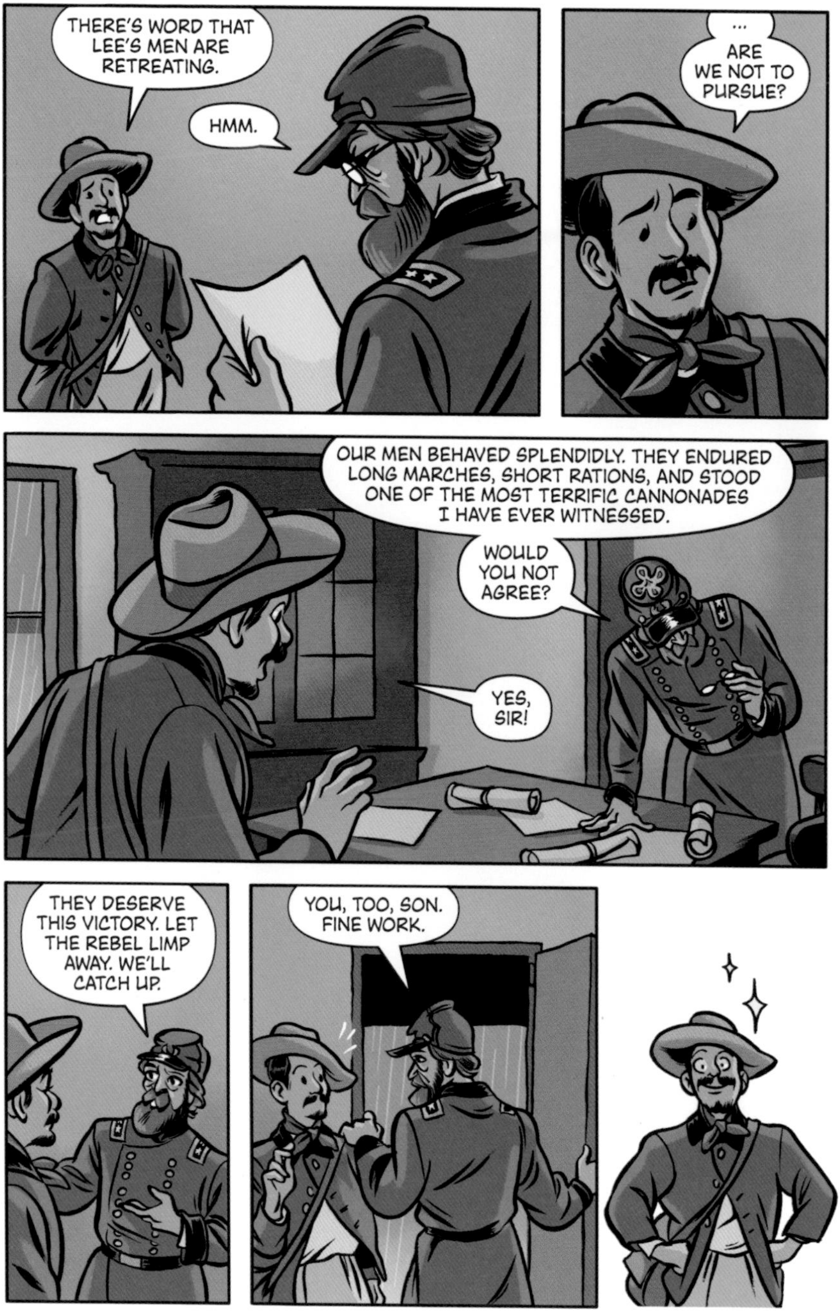
THERE'S WORD THAT LEE'S MEN ARE RETREATING.
HMM.
...
ARE WE NOT TO PURSUE?
OUR MEN BEHAVED SPLENDIDLY. THEY ENDURED LONG MARCHES, SHORT RATIONS, AND STOOD ONE OF THE MOST TERRIFIC CANNONADES I HAVE EVER WITNESSED.
WOULD YOU NOT AGREE?
YES, SIR!
THEY DESERVE THIS VICTORY. LET THE REBEL LIMP AWAY. WE'LL CATCH UP.
YOU, TOO, SON. FINE WORK.

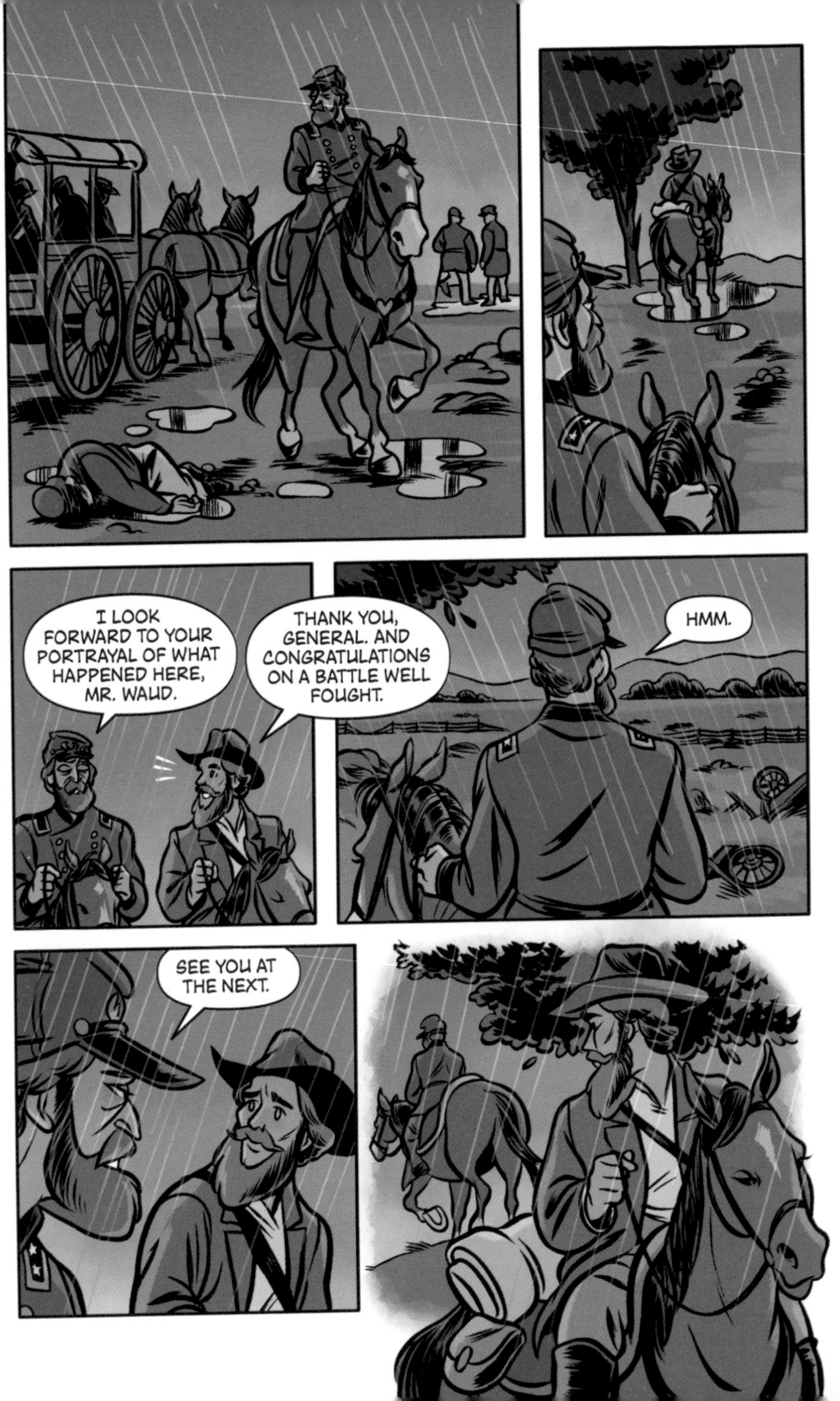
I LOOK FORWARD TO YOUR PORTRAYAL OF WHAT HAPPENED HERE, MR. WAUD.
THANK YOU, GENERAL. AND CONGRATULATIONS ON A BATTLE WELL FOUGHT.
HMM.
SEE YOU AT THE NEXT.

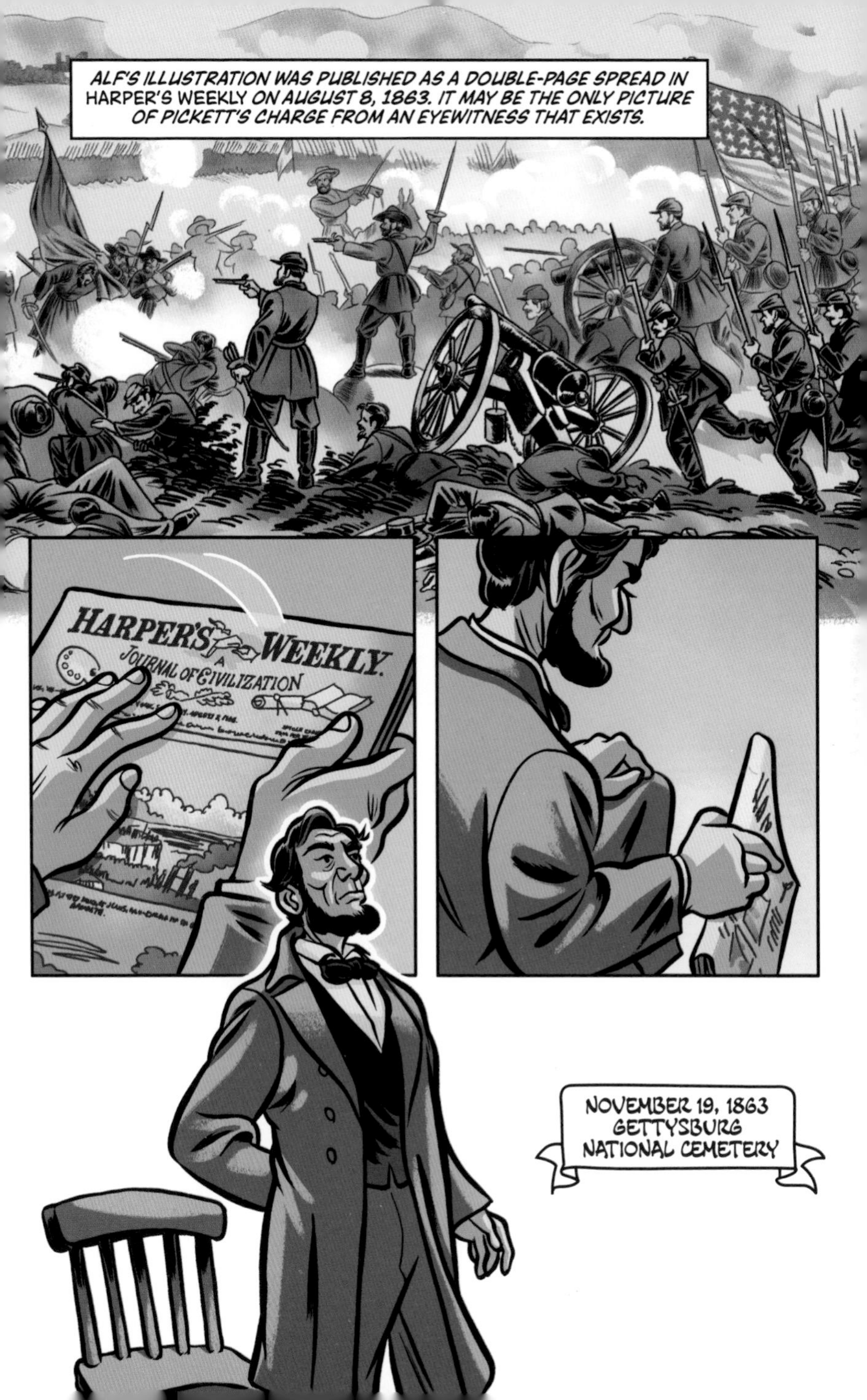
ALF'S ILLUSTRATION WAS PUBLISHED AS A DOUBLE-PAGE SPREAD IN HARPER'S WEEKLY ON AUGUST 8, 1863. IT MAY BE THE ONLY PICTURE OF PICKETT'S CHARGE FROM AN EYEWITNESS THAT EXISTS.
HARPER'S WEEKLY.
A JOURNAL OF CIVILIZATION
NOVEMBER 19, 1863
GETTYSBURG
NATIONAL CEMETERY

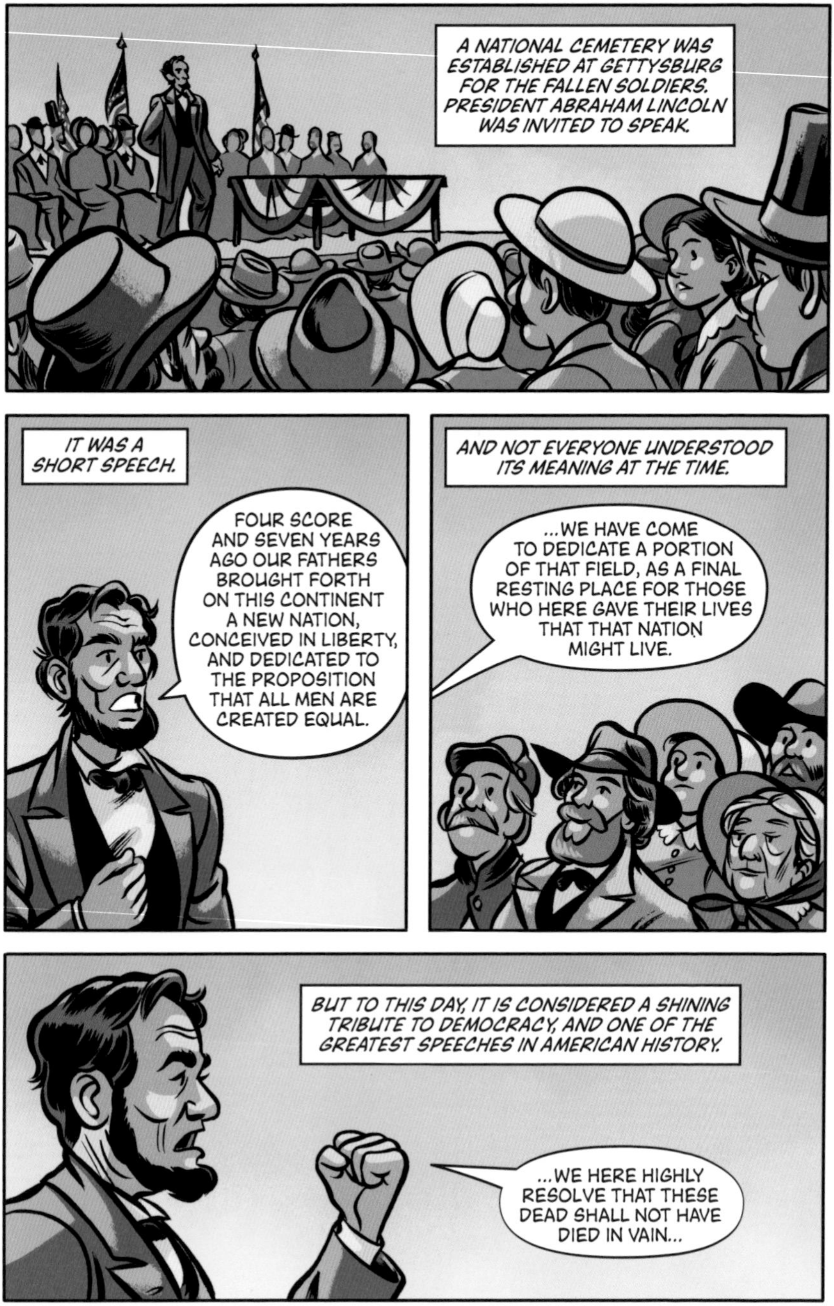
A NATIONAL CEMETERY WAS ESTABLISHED AT GETTYSBURG FOR THE FALLEN SOLDIERS. PRESIDENT ABRAHAM LINCOLN WAS INVITED TO SPEAK.
IT WAS A SHORT SPEECH.
FOUR SCORE AND SEVEN YEARS AGO OUR FATHERS BROUGHT FORTH ON THIS CONTINENT A NEW NATION, CONCEIVED IN LIBERTY, AND DEDICATED TO THE PROPOSITION THAT ALL MEN ARE CREATED EQUAL.
AND NOT EVERYONE UNDERSTOOD ITS MEANING AT THE TIME.
...WE HAVE COME TO DEDICATE A PORTION OF THAT FIELD, AS A FINAL RESTING PLACE FOR THOSE WHO HERE GAVE THEIR LIVES THAT THAT NATION MIGHT LIVE.
BUT TO THIS DAY, IT IS CONSIDERED A SHINING TRIBUTE TO DEMOCRACY, AND ONE OF THE GREATEST SPEECHES IN AMERICAN HISTORY.
...WE HERE HIGHLY RESOLVE THAT THESE DEAD SHALL NOT HAVE DIED IN VAIN...

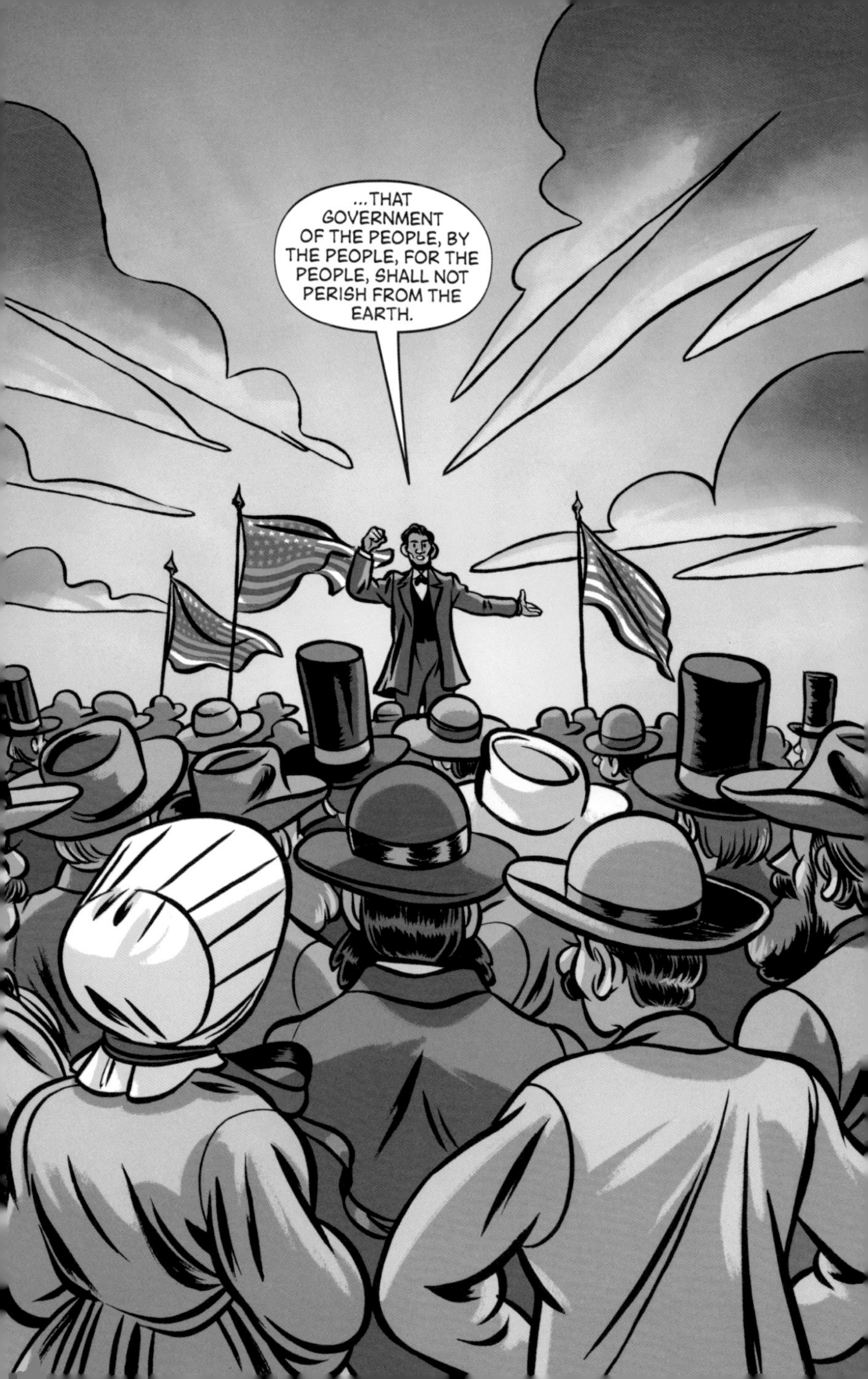
...THAT GOVERNMENT OF THE PEOPLE, BY THE PEOPLE, FOR THE PEOPLE, SHALL NOT PERISH FROM THE EARTH.

Conclusion

President Lincoln looked out over the graves of thousands—soldiers who had given their lives to defend their country. On that crisp November day, he dedicated not only himself, but every American to the promise of a nation based on liberty and equality. He called it "unfinished work," because the war was not over and there was much to be done.

Alfred R. Waud followed the Union army until the day General Lee surrendered, on April 9, 1865. He faithfully illustrated every battle and helped keep a nation of readers informed of the war. The special artist as a profession did not last long, giving way to photography and later television for war correspondence. However, Alf would be remembered for his bravery, for his talent, and for conveying truth above all.

Lincoln welcomed Southern secessionists back into the Union with open arms. Still, some were not willing to give up the false idea that white people were a superior race, also known as white supremacy. Years after the war, former Confederates began to spread a false history called the Lost Cause. According to the Lost Cause, the Confederacy did not fight for the right to own enslaved people, but for states' rights to govern the way they wanted. They also claimed that

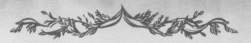

formerly enslaved people were better off as property of white people. These were white supremacist lies, but they were told as facts, even taught in Southern schools. Many Americans believe this false history to this day.

Today, activists dedicated to civil rights are working to correct the false history of the Lost Cause, including foundations like the Institute for Southern Studies and the National Association for the Advancement of Colored People (NAACP). They are continuing the nation's unfinished work—the promise of liberty and equality for all Americans.

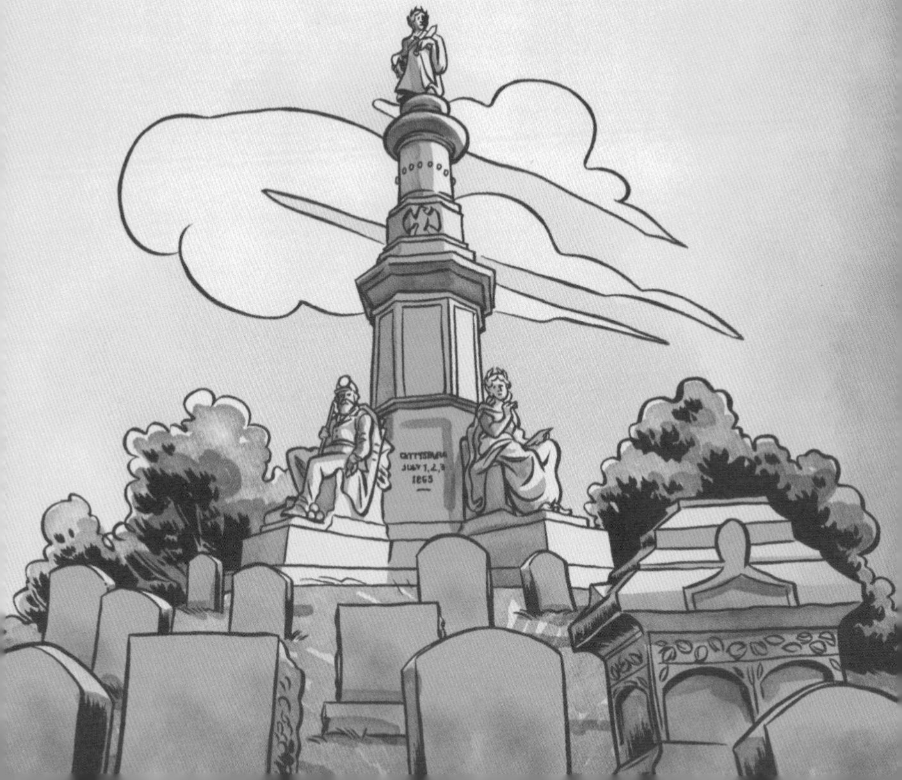

Timeline of the Battle of Gettysburg

1860 — Abraham Lincoln is elected president of the United States

— Confederate States of America form

1861 — The Civil War begins

— Alfred Waud goes to Washington, DC, on assignment as a special artist to accompany the Union army

1862 — The Confederates defeat the Union in Fredericksburg, Virginia

1863 — President Lincoln issues the Emancipation Proclamation on January 1, freeing all enslaved people in Rebel states

— General George G. Meade is appointed commander of the Union Army of the Potomac on June 28

— The Battle of Gettysburg begins on July 1

— General Lee and his Confederate army retreat on July 4

— The Gettysburg Campaign officially ends on July 14, when General Lee and his men escape over the Potomac River, back into Southern territory

— President Lincoln delivers the Gettysburg Address on November 19

1919 — The Rutherford Committee is established to promote the Lost Cause in school textbooks in the United States

Bibliography

*Books for young readers

Blackett, R. J. M., ed. *Thomas Morris Chester, Black Civil War Correspondent: His Dispatches from the Virginia Front.* Baton Rouge: Louisiana State University Press, 1989. https://archive.org/details/thomasmorrischesooooches.

Haskell, Frank A. "Haskell's Account of the Battle of Gettysburg." In *American Historical Documents, 1000–1904, Vol. XLIII, The Harvard Classics,* edited by Charles W. Eliot. New York: P. F. Collier & Son, 1909–14. http://www.bartleby.com/43/3501.html.

Holzer, Harold, ed. *Hearts Touched By Fire: The Best of Battles and Leaders of the Civil War.* New York: Modern Library, 2011.

Huffman, Greg. "Twisted Sources: How Confederate Propaganda Ended Up in the South's Schoolbooks." *Facing South,* April 10, 2019. http://www.facingsouth.org/2019/04/twisted-sources-how-confederate-propaganda-ended-souths-schoolbooks.

Kagan, Neil, Harris J. Andrews, and Paula York-Soderlund, ed. *Great Battles of the Civil War: An Illustrated History of Courage Under Fire.* Birmingham, AL: Oxmoor House, 2002.

LaFantasie, Glenn W. *Twilight at Little Round Top: July 2, 1863—The Tide Turns at Gettysburg.* Hoboken, NJ: John Wiley & Sons, 2005.

*O'Connor, Jim. *What Was the Battle of Gettysburg?* New York: Penguin Workshop, 2013.

Ray, Frederic E. *"Our Special Artist": Alfred R. Waud's Civil War.* Mechanicsburg, PA: Stackpole Books, 1994.

ABOUT THE CREATOR

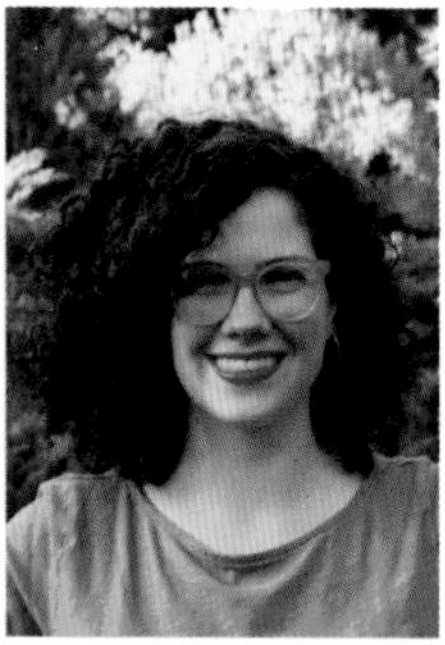

Ellen T. Crenshaw is an award-winning cartoonist and illustrator for books, editorial, comics, and children's media. Her first graphic novel, *Kiss Number 8*, was longlisted for the 2019 National Book Award and nominated for the 2020 Eisner Award. She lives in California with her husband, Night Fury, and razorback sand terrier. Find her at ellencrenshaw.com.